I KNOW
ABSOLUTELY
NOTHING
A B O U T™
TENNIS

A Tennis Player's Guide to the
Sport's History, Equipment,
Apparel, Etiquette,
Rules, and Language

Tracy Austin and Steve Eubanks

Rutledge Hill Press
Nashville, Tennessee

Published in Nashville, Tennessee, by Rutledge Hill Press, 211 Seventh Avenue North, Nashville, Tennessee 37219.

Distributed in Canada by H. B. Fenn & Company, Ltd., 34 Nixon Road, Bolton, Ontario L7E 1W2.

Distributed in Australia by Millennium Books, 33 Maddox Street, Alexandria NSW 2015.

Distributed in New Zealand by Tandem Press, 2 Rugby Road, Birkenhead, Auckland 10.

Distributed in the United Kingdom by Verulam Publishing, Ltd., 152a Park Street Lane, Park Street, St. Albans, Hertfordshire AL2 2AU.

Typography by D&T Bailey Typesetting, Inc., Nashville, Tennessee

Inside illustrations by David Alden

ISBN: 1-55853-497-0

Printed in the United States of America

1   2   3   4   5   6   7   8   9—00 99   98   97

CONTENTS

ACKNOWLEDGMENTS

Few people outside the industry appreciate all the pieces that must fall into place for an idea to transform into bound, printed pages. This book would not be a reality without the selfless efforts of some outstanding people. Among them: our illustrator, David Alden, who has once again created some of the most imaginative and memorable "notes" ever put on paper; Brian Albert and Teresa Anderson of Advantage International, who brought us together and sparked what has become a burgeoning friendship; Larry Stone, publisher and friend, who shares our vision for the future; Mike Towle, editor, friend, and a champion of all the *I Know Absolutely Nothing About*™ books. Special thanks to Dennis Rizza, Kim Perino, and all the staff and friends at the Kramer Club for their technical assistance and advice. Also, thanks to John Austin for his help. And as always, a deeply held love and heartfelt thanks to our spouses and families for their support throughout this process. We could not have done it without them.

INTRODUCTION

When we first began work on this project, we wondered how two people from such opposite ends of the tennis spectrum were ever going to collaborate and find one voice. After all, one of us has won two U.S. Open singles titles and the other has had trouble winning against the ball machine. But it didn't take us long to realize that this is exactly what the *I Know Absolutely Nothing About*™ books are all about. We quickly discovered that not only do novices experience overwhelming embarrassment at their ignorance, so do players who have been in the game almost their entire lives. Perhaps those in the latter category take certain knowledge and information for granted, assuming (wrongly) that they already know all pertinent words and phrases. What we learned from working together is that nothing should be taken for granted in teaching about tennis.

That's why our main character in *I Know Absolutely Nothing about Tennis* might come across as somewhat naive. No one living in the twentieth century and owning a television set should be quite as clueless as our Stacy. But by placing her in the role of total neophyte, we have, we hope, crafted an enjoyable tale that covers all the basics in tennis. Fair warning: Don't expect to read this book and win major tennis events because of it. What you can expect is that you will learn all the things you need to begin your journey into the wonderful world of tennis. From where to go, what to buy, how to dress, what to ask, and what to expect, this book prepares you for your first experiences on the court. It should help eliminate the anxiety you will likely feel the first time you step onto a tennis court in white shorts or miniskirt with all eyes seemingly on you.

As with all *I Know Absolutely Nothing About*™ books, don't expect your local tennis shop or club to give you the kind of sycophantic service accorded our fictitious Stacy. Tennis professionals typically are helpful and courteous, but they are busy people who probably don't have an entire day to devote to you. That's why we wrote this book. By placing our character in an almost-surreal setting, we let her ask all the questions you are too anxious or embarrassed to ask. And remember, the stupidest questions are the ones never asked.

We can't promise to make you play better, but we are sure you will have a great time. Play well!

—*Tracy Austin and Steve Eubanks*

ONE

HARD COURTSHIP

Stacy is going out of her mind. She stares out the living room window and dusts her favorite end table for the tenth time. The floors have been done, and the last of the moving boxes went out in this morning's trash. A television talk show provides background noise, and Stacy half-listens as the discussion turns to "new town blues—struggling with the pressures and depression of moving."

Stacy and Matt have been in town for six weeks now, and while she loves her new house and Matt loves his new job, Stacy doesn't know anyone. Her nearest friend lives five hundred miles away, and with Matt working extra hours these first few weeks, she has become a reclusive prisoner in their charming white hillside cottage. The last three weeks have been an endless series of television talk shows, trips to the grocer, house-straightening chores, and long-distance phone calls to friends and family who are willing to commiserate with her.

She has to do something to meet people or she's going to go bonkers.

The phone rings, and Stacy leaps for it.

"Hi, honey, it's me," Matt announces. From the background noise, Stacy can tell he's calling from his new office.

"Oh, hi," Stacy replies in a deflated tone.

"Gee, it's good to hear you, too."

"I'm sorry, Matt. It's just that I've worked on the computer this morning, read all the books and magazines in the house, and now I'm dusting the same piece of furniture and watching talk shows again. I'm bored to tears. You know people at work, but I don't know anybody."

"I know, honey. Can't you go out and meet some of the neighbors?" Matt asks, and then turns away from the phone to speak to a passing coworker.

Stacy's voice cracks and tears well up in her eyes. "You don't understand at all, do you? What do you want me to do, walk up to a neighbor and say, 'Hi, we just moved in and I'm bored'? I can't do that."

"I'm sorry, Stacy," Matt reacts, immediately aware that his lack of sensitivity just added to the problem. "Look, I think I've got the answer. It's a month away, but I've entered us in a mixed doubles tennis tournament that the company puts on every year. Everybody from the office will be there with their spouses. You'll meet a lot of people and—"

"You what?" Stacy yells into the phone. "I'm telling you that I'm losing my mind here, and you

try to cheer me up by telling me you've entered us in a tennis tournament! I know absolutely nothing about tennis. Nothing! How am I supposed to play a tournament in a month? I don't even know where to start. I can't believe you'd do this. Count me out."

"Stacy, relax, lots of beginners play in this thing. According to Sam, it's more of a social gathering than a tournament. Nobody's out for blood or glory."

"Yeah, right," she snaps.

"Look, you'll be fine. You're a good athlete, and this is a great opportunity for you to meet everyone."

Stacy takes a deep breath. The anxiety she's feeling isn't Matt's fault, and she knows she shouldn't throw all this onto him. "I'm sorry, Matt," she concedes.

"It's okay, honey. I'm sorry, too. I know you're bored and stressed out from the move, but this is a great chance for you to meet everybody and make some friends."

"I know it is," she says. "Go ahead and leave us on the list. I'll do the best I can."

Stacy tells Matt she loves him, then hangs up the phone. A wave of anxiety passes over her as she considers what she's just committed to. In one month she's going to meet all of Matt's coworkers—his boss, his friends, the infamous Sam he talks so much about. She's in a new town and her first interaction with her husband's company will be playing a game she knows absolutely nothing about.

Stacy needs some air. It's a beautiful day, so she grabs the car keys and heads out. A good drive always helps her to clear her head and put things into perspective. Stacy turns left out of her neighborhood, and two blocks away, she makes another turn down a street she's never seen. The houses along this stretch are pretty, and she slows to look at the landscaping along some of the driveways. Then something else catches her eye: At the end of the street, at least twenty cars are parked in front of a large building. As Stacy draws closer, she sees a sign: Saddle Ridge Tennis Center.

Curiosity forces her to turn into the lot. Beyond the clubhouse she sees two groups of women, each group dressed in matching skirts and tops. Both groups are gathered around one of the many surrounding tennis courts as four women hit balls back and forth over a net. Stacy assumes this is a tournament, or team event, or something. With nothing to do the rest of the afternoon, Stacy resolves to put an end to her anxiety and her ignorance. She is not going to let Matt down. She is going to learn tennis.

A door on one side of the clubhouse displays the legend Pro Shop. Also posted on the door is a sign-up sheet for Today's League Matches. Stacy notes that twenty-four people signed up for today. When she opens the pro shop door, the first thing she notices is a wall full of racquets with no strings. The hollow frames seem unusually large to her, and she wonders why the strings are missing.

"May I help you?"

Startled, Stacy turns to see a young woman with blonde hair and a broad smile wearing a stylish warm-up suit over a casual sports shirt. "Hi," Stacy responds, extending her hand to the lady. "My name's Stacy. I really hope you can help me."

"I'll try, Stacy. My name is Stephanie Griff. What can I do for you?"

"Well, I was driving through and saw the tennis courts. You see, my husband and I are new in town. We moved here about six weeks ago. Anyway, my husband's office has this tennis tournament in a month. He signed me up so I can meet all his coworkers, which would be great except I know absolutely nothing about tennis. I mean, I know nothing."

"And you have one month to learn enough to play in a tournament," Stephanie says.

"And, hopefully not humiliate myself in front of my husband's entire office staff," Stacy finishes.

The young lady's smile grows larger. "You're certainly in the right place," she announces. "We have one of the most active tennis facilities in the state."

"Would you have time to help me?" Stacy asks.

"Sure," Stephanie says. "In fact, I've got time this afternoon. Step back into my office and we'll get started."

Two

Tennis 101

Stephanie's office is a small room in the corner of the pro shop. Her cluttered desk is surrounded by walls filled with posters of sweat-drenched tennis players in the heat of battle. Stacy assumes these are pictures of some of the best players in the world. She also assumes, from the tennis bag sitting on the floor beside the desk and various trophies adorning shelf space in the office, that Stephanie is a very good player in her own right.

"I take it those are yours," Stacy observes.

Stephanie nods. "I keep the others at home. They aren't GRAND SLAM titles by any means, but I'm still competitive."

Stacy makes a mental note to ask what Grand Slam titles are. "Well, Stephanie, I hope you know what you've gotten yourself into. I wasn't kidding when I said I know absolutely nothing about tennis. I don't know the rules; I don't even know the objectives."

"It's easy," Stephanie assures her. "Two or four players, each with a racquet, hit a ball back and forth over a net and into a rectangular court. If you hit the ball over the net and into the court one more time than your opponent you win a POINT. If you win enough points you win a GAME, and if you win enough games you win the MATCH."

Stacy nods. That sounds easy enough. "So, you've been playing a long time?"

"Oh, as long as I can remember. My parents put a racquet in my hands when I was three years old, and I've been hooked on the game ever since. One of the great things about tennis is that there are no age limits—whether you're three or ninety-three you can still enjoy the competition and health benefits."

Pondering her next question, Stacy notices another picture on a shelf behind Stephanie's desk. Unlike the posters, this small framed photo, black-and-white and faded from age, is of a man playing tennis in slacks and a tie. The racquet he's holding is smaller than the ones in the shop, and it looks to Stacy as if it's made of wood.

"Is that a relative of yours?" she inquires.

Stephanie looks back at the picture and chuckles. "Oh, no. That man's name is William Renshaw. He dominated men's play and won seven Wimbledon singles championships in the 1880s."

"He looks uncomfortable," Stacy comments, noting the somewhat formal attire.

Stephanie nods, explaining, "Back in those days proper attire was part of the ritual. Comfort was secondary, if it was considered at all. Today at public parks you can see anything.

"There weren't any public park players back in William's day. The big public park push wasn't until the 1960s. Before then, tennis was a club sport played primarily on private courts. In the early days tennis was a game for the aristocracy. It wasn't until much later that it became a game for the masses."

Stacy reaches into her purse and pulls out a notepad she always carries. She figures this is information she'd better write down. "When was tennis first established?" she asks, pen and pad in hand.

"Well, that's a matter of much debate. The modern game is just over a century old, relatively young by standards of other similar sports; but the precursors of tennis, games like real or royal tennis, were played for hundreds of years. Court sizes varied and the rules were often made up as they went along. It wasn't until a December afternoon in 1873 that an English gentleman named Major Walter Wingfield introduced a new garden party game he called Sphairistike, or Sticky."

"Spare-what?" Stacy asks.

"Sphairistike [sfair-is-TEEK]," Stephanie says. "It's a Greek word that means 'ball game,' but even in those days people couldn't pronounce it or remember it, so it quickly became sticky. Shortly after that it became known as lawn tennis.

"The first tennis courts were actually modified croquet lawns. Major Wingfield loved party games and he had played different variations of royal tennis, so he decided to standardize a very old game and give it a new name and some new rules. He was a great promoter so it came as no surprise to the people who knew him when the good Major began advertising and promoting what he called 'tennis sets,' which included balls, racquets, rules, and special shoes with India-rubber soles. He even sold special 'sphairistike tape measures' so that the net would always be strung accurately and according to his rules."

"Sounds like he was a pretty savvy salesman," Stacy remarks.

"You bet," Stephanie laughs. "He even tried to convince people that lawn tennis could be played in the winter on ice skates. Needless to say, that didn't go over very well.

"Don't get me wrong," Stephanie continues, "the game really owes its popularity to Major Wingfield. He recognized that tennis wasn't just an English sport, and within a decade it had spread throughout the world. By 1874 the game had arrived in the United States. A lady named Mary Outerbridge introduced it to the Staten Island Baseball and Cricket Club."

"A woman brought the game to America? Good for her," Stacy pronounces.

"Yeah, she was a well-kept woman who spent her winters in Bermuda," Stephanie adds. "As the story goes, in March of 1874, after seeing military personnel play this new game, she returned home, but when her ship landed in New York Harbor she was detained because customs agents had no idea what the tennis racquets and balls in her luggage were. When you think about it, the spread of tennis is really quite remarkable."

Stacy feverishly writes all this down, then she glances back up at Stephanie's trophies. "So when did tennis go beyond a garden party game?" she asks.

"Good question." Stephanie leans forward and puts her elbows on her desk. "In 1875 the All England Croquet Club, located in Wimbledon, committed one of its lawns to tennis, and two years later it hosted the very first tennis tournament. The event was called the Lawn Tennis Championships at the All England Croquet and Lawn Tennis Club."

"Wimbledon," Stacy comments. "I've heard of that. It's still a big tournament, right?"

"One of the biggest," Stephanie says. "WIMBLEDON, along with the FRENCH OPEN, the AUSTRALIAN OPEN, and the U.S. OPEN constitute tennis's GRAND SLAM. The tournaments are sometimes called majors or just Grand Slam events.

"There's a lot of tradition and reverence about the All England Club and the Wimbledon championships, but in those early days it was a little different. The first Wimbledon champion, a man named Spencer Gore, said that 'any gamesplayer worth his sweat wouldn't find tennis a satisfactory pastime.'"

"I guess they didn't retire his number, or whatever they do in tennis," Stacy remarks with a smile.

Stephanie laughs. "No, but Gore's comments were nothing. In the 1879 tournament, Reverend John Hartley won his semifinal match, left Wimbledon,

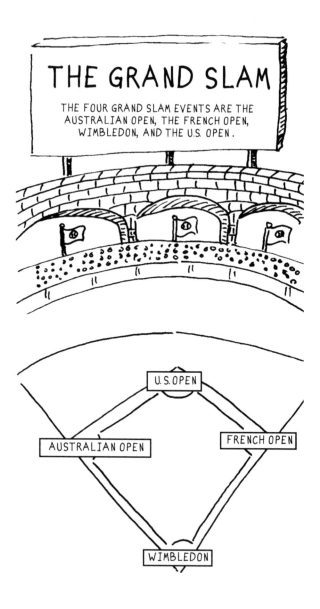

and drove his carriage all the way to Yorkshire where he presided over Sunday services at his church. He then loaded back up in his carriage, drove back to Wimbledon, and on Monday won the championship. The man Hartley defeated in that Wimbledon final, Leger Gould, was later sentenced to life on Devil's Island after he murdered a Danish woman and hid her dismembered body in his luggage."

"True story?" Stacy asks.

"Scout's honor," Stephanie says.

Stacy looks again at the posters adorning the walls. "Do those players qualify as great players?" she wants to know.

"You bet," Stephanie affirms as she leans back in her chair and points to the posters. She notes a few of today's champions, who include:

- Michael Chang, who has won the French Open and was the youngest player in history to win a main draw match at the U.S. Open;
- Pete Sampras, who has won more than forty-five singles titles and is one of only three players ever to be ranked number one for four or more consecutive years;
- Steffi Graf of Germany, winner of more than one hundred tour titles;
- Boris Becker, another German, who is the youngest man to win the Wimbledon singles title;
- Monica Seles, who has won more than forty career titles and has been ranked number one in the world;

- Arantxa Sanchez Vicario, the first Spanish player ever to hold a number-one singles ranking;
- Andre Agassi, who has won more than thirty-five career titles and is considered the reigning king of cutting-edge style among top-ranked players.

Stacy fills up a page in her notepad, then questions, "Has anyone ever won all the Grand Slam tournaments in one year?"

"Actually, it's been done six times in singles competition. In 1938 Californian Don Budge won all four majors and became the first man to capture tennis's Grand Slam. Others who have since won the SLAM are Maureen Connolly (1953), Australian Rod Laver (twice, 1962 and 1969), Margaret Court Smith, also an Aussie (1970), and, most recently (through 1996), Steffi Graf (1988). Maureen, better known as 'Little Mo,' held the record as the youngest player ever to win a U.S. Open until Tracy Austin won in 1979 at the ripe old age of sixteen years, nine months, edging Connolly's record by two months. You've probably heard of Tracy Austin."

Stacy attentively writes all this down while Stephanie goes on to tell her that Grand Slam events are run by the ITF, the INTERNATIONAL TENNIS FEDERATION, which also runs the Davis Cup and Fed Cup, tennis's international team competitions for men and women. She also gives Stacy an overview of other great players throughout history, including some of the greatest who ever played:

- Bill Tilden, who dominated the game in the 1920s;
- Jack Kramer, a Southern California athlete who took tennis to a new level after World War II;
- René Lacoste, who twice won Wimbledon, the French Open, and the U.S. Open championships, but who is more widely known for the line of sports clothing that bears his name (and the logo of his nickname, "the Crocodile");
- Helen Jacobs, who won four straight U.S. Opens;
- Gussy Moran, who created quite a stir when she wore lace panties at Wimbledon. The pants, designed by sports designer Ted Tinling, are mild by today's standards of protocol, but in 1949 they created a huge controversy and were seen as not just risqué and undignified, but sinful.

"Tennis history is full of great stories and great champions. When you get into the sport, you probably will read about some of the greats and what they've accomplished. Names like Pancho Gonzalez, Arthur Ashe, Billie Jean King, Althea Gibson, Jimmy Connors, Chris Evert, Martina Navratilova, Bjorn Borg, and John McEnroe, to name a few."

Stacy looks back at the list that she has written down. "You said some of these players were 'ranked' number one. Ranked by whom?"

"Great question. Professionals in tennis are ranked by the WTA, which stands for WOMEN'S TENNIS

ASSOCIATION, and the ATP, which stands for the AS-
SOCIATION OF TENNIS PROFESSIONALS. The rankings
are all done by computer and they can change each
week since the computer calculates rankings based
on the previous fifty-two-week period. These rankings are very important because professional events
seed players according to their rankings—"

"Whoa," Stacy interrupts. "Did you say they seed
them, like planting a seed?"

Stephanie chuckles. "Sorry, I didn't mean to get
ahead of you. Yes, SEED is a term used to describe
where a player is placed in a tournament. Let's say a
tournament starts off with thirty-two participants.
To get to a winner, you have to divide that field in
half, or into brackets, and have players in each
bracket play a succession of 'surviving' opponents
until you only have one player left in each half.
Those two players then play in what's called the finals. Players are seeded in such a way as to avoid
having the field's best players meet one another in
an early round.

"Back in 1924 the folks at the All England Club
decided to deliberately place the top-ranked players
in certain brackets to keep the best players away
from each other until the late rounds. That was
called seeding, and it's now the standard in professional tournaments. The number-one- and number-
two-ranked players are placed in different halves,
and other top players are placed in separate brackets
so high-ranking players don't play each other until
the late rounds, say the quarterfinals or semifinals.

A top-seeded player is the highest-ranked player in a given tournament. If the number-one player in the world enters an event, he or she is the top seed."

"So the ranking and seeding are done by com-puter," Stacy states, just to make sure she understands.

Stephanie goes on to say that while all four Grand Slam events have the right to seed competi-tors on their own, Wimbledon is usually the only one of the four not to seed exactly by the computer. She explains, "Certain players are more adept at play-ing the grass courts of Wimbledon, so it would make sense that the tournament committee determine the seeding. Which brings up another interesting point. There's some debate about the computer ranking system, because a few players won't play on courts or surfaces where they don't play well in order to retain their ranking. If you don't play, you don't lose; ergo you have a better chance of keeping your ranking."

"That doesn't seem right," Stacy objects.

Stephanie agrees. "The vast majority of profes-sionals don't play those kinds of games, so, overall, the computer ranking system works pretty well."

Stacy realizes that while this is great information to know, she's not a lot closer to learning how to ac-tually play the game than she was when she arrived. "Is there an organization that ranks players who know absolutely nothing?"

Stephanie nods. "There is a nationally recog-nized system for ranking amateurs who want to play in leagues or community events, or who just want to find an equitable social game."

"That's me," Stacy admits.

"Okay," Stephanie says, "when you show up at your husband's tournament, how are you going to know the people you're playing are close to the same skill level as you?"

"Look for the person walking with crutches," Stacy says.

Stephanie laughs. "The NATIONAL TENNIS RATING PROGRAM has a set of standards to rate players according to their ability levels. The NTRP system rates players numerically from a 2.5 (beginners who have certain basic skills) all the way to 7.0 (the best players in the world). This system is just a way of pairing people who have similar skills. If you are a 2.5 player, you wouldn't want to play a 7.0 player.

"As far as joining any other associations, the best advice I can give is, once you've learned the basics and feel comfortable playing at some level, look into joining a league. We have a number of league events at this club."

Stacy remembers the women in their uniforms and the sign-up sheet she saw on the pro shop door. "What kind of league are we talking about here? I mean, I'm not even bush league at this point."

"You don't have to be a world-class player to play in a league," Stephanie assures her. "In fact, leagues are the fastest way for you to grow in the sport while meeting people. Anyone with an NTRP rating can join a league, and most clubs and public park departments can put you in touch with league coordinators."

WTA = WOMEN'S TENNIS ASSOCIATION

ATP = ASSOCIATION OF TENNIS
PROFESSIONALS (MEN)

NATIONAL TENNIS RATING PROGRAM

2.5 - WORST
(BEGINNER)

3.0 - BAD

3.5

4.0 - NOT SO BAD

4.5

5.0 - BETTER
(TOP CLUB PLAYERS)

5.5

6.0 - GOOD

6.5

7.0 - BEST
(WORLD-CLASS)

"I don't know if I'm ready for that yet," Stacy demurs.

"Don't worry," Stephanie reassures. "Before you know it, you'll be charging the NET and slamming winners. Now, there's someone on our staff I'd like you to meet."

"Lead the way," Stacy says.

Out in the pro shop Stephanie speaks to a group of women who have just finished their matches. There's great camaraderie among the group as they relay details of their play to Stephanie, who listens patiently. While the conversation progresses, Stacy wanders over to a corner of the shop where a man has taken one of the stringless racquet frames off the wall. She watches as the man places the frame on a menacing-looking machine.

"Hello," the man greets her. "Are you here with the league?"

"Oh, no," she replies. "I'm here with the ignorant. I know absolutely nothing about tennis and I'm here trying to learn enough to get started."

The man looks up from his machine. "That's great," he declares through a widening smile. "You've certainly come to the right place."

"You said it," Stephanie affirms, joining them. "Red, this is Stacy, our student for the day."

The man extends a large athletic hand to Stacy. "Red Lever," he says. "It's nice to have you."

"It's nice to be here," Stacy responds. She now notices that Red has the wiry build of a runner and the wind-worn face of a man who spends a lot of time outdoors.

"Red is our equipment manager and professional stringer, that is, when he's not out winning tournaments," Stephanie explains.

Red smiles and blushes. "No wins lately," he says.

"Oh, you're a professional?" Stacy asks.

"Of sorts," Red acknowledges. "I still play in a few events."

"Don't let him kid you," Stephanie jumps in. "Red's been nationally ranked and is still one of the top players in his age group. So, Red, can you spend a little time with Stacy on racquets?" Stephanie asks, then returns her attention to Stacy. "I assume you don't own a racquet."

"I don't own one, nor do I know anything about them," Stacy concedes.

"Well, Red's your man. He knows as much about racquets and equipment as anyone in the business."

"I hope you're up for a challenge," Stacy says to Red.

"Always," Red answers.

THREE

EXPLAIN THIS RACQUET

"It seems obvious, but in order to play tennis you need a tennis racquet," Red begins. "However, unlike other sports such as skiing, golf, and scuba diving, tennis is relatively inexpensive for a beginner. Once you buy a racquet, assuming you own a pair of tennis shoes and some loose-fitting clothing, the only other expenses you have are tennis balls and court rental."

Stacy has her notepad out, and she underlines the word *inexpensive*. Given her reservations about her aptitude, this is an important point.

Red continues his explanation: "Racquets have a number of different components, each of which affects performance and has a bearing on your ability to improve." He takes down one of the many racquet frames that hang on the wall.

"Why doesn't it have strings?" Stacy asks.

"Good question. You can buy a pre-strung racquet at almost any sports store, or you can buy a frame and have a tennis pro string the racquet for you. Stringing is one of many variables that affect performance. Depending on your style of play and the goals you want to achieve, proper stringing will be a factor in your ability to improve."

"My goals are modest and I don't have a style of play," Stacy admits.

Red smiles at this and continues. "That's why there are tennis professionals. I strongly recommend you spend time with a teaching pro before buying a racquet. Once you've learned a few basics, you'll see that buying a frame that works and having your racquet strung by a professional are the smart way to go."

Stacy writes this down and worries about making the right choices. "You said there were a lot of components to buying a racquet. What are the important ones?"

"They're all important, but before you can make an intelligent buying decision, you have to understand the different parts of a racquet and how each part affects performance." He then explains that racquets can be divided into three main parts:

- the HEAD, which is the large oval end of the racquet where the strings are woven;
- the SHAFT, which is the portion of the racquet that connects the head with the grip;
- the GRIP, which is wrapped with either leather or a synthetic material to provide softer feel and to cushion the vibration that comes from hitting a tennis ball.

Stacy examines the racquet and notices that the

shaft is actually V-shaped and open in the center. "Why does the shaft of that racquet split into a V?"

Red holds the racquet by the head. "This is what's known as a composite graphite racquet, because it's made from a graphite material." He goes on to say that tennis technology has advanced to a point where racquets are made from all kinds of materials, including:

- composite plastics,
- fiberglass,
- injection and compression molded graphites,
- kevlar, which is material used in bullet-proof vests,
- ceramics,
- and even titanium.

"The term *shaft,* while still applicable, is a holdover from the days when all racquets were made of wood," Red concludes.

Stacy remembers the wooden racquet in the old photo of William Renshaw behind Stephanie's desk and mentions it to Red.

"The change in technology has been relatively sudden," Red explains. "From the late 1800s until the early 1980s almost all tennis racquets were made of wood. Now almost none are. In fact, former great René Lacoste, who also founded and marketed his own line of sports clothes bearing his crocodile logo, actually developed the first steel racquet and sold it to a major manufacturer (Wilson). But steel's reception by the industry was slow until Billie Jean King won Wimbledon and the

U.S. Open in the late 1960s playing with the steel racquet. Still, it was another fifteen years before the transition was complete and wooden racquets were put away for good. Today's composite materials are stronger, lighter, and more durable than ever. In the old days, for example, a player might actually break a racquet every couple of months. Now, you'd need a blowtorch to break a titanium racquet. The materials are more dense than wood while still being lighter, so if you made a graphite racquet the same weight as an old wooden racquet, you could use it as a chin-up bar. Technology is progressing so fast that every year a new and improved racquet design hits the market."

"Just what I need," Stacy sighs. "I'll be out of style before I even get started."

Red chuckles. "The most important thing to remember about all tennis racquets is to pick one you like and one that feels comfortable to you. It's very easy to get mired in all the new gizmos, and lose sight of your primary objective, which is learning to play.

"Now, back to your question about the shaft," Red continues. "Composite materials have allowed manufacturers to modify racquet designs, making the heads bigger and the overall weight much lighter. Part of that new design has been to split the shaft and create an open throat in the racquet."

He points to the open area of the V between the head and the grip.

"The bottom portion of the head is called the BRIDGE," Red says, running his hand inside the V along the smooth surface of the head. He then points to the connecting arms of the V near where they touch the racquet head, saying, "The SHOULDERS are the link between the head, the bridge, and the shaft. The design of the shoulders and the throat have a great deal to do with the flex and torque of the racquet. This might not seem important to you now, but it's a critical element in playing good tennis."

Stacy eventually wants to play well, so she dutifully makes notes and does her best to draw all the different parts of the racquet Red has described.

"This particular racquet has what's known as an OVERWRAP or GRIP WRAP," Red adds as he points to the grip. "This is an additional wrap placed over the grip either to make the grip bigger or to provide a softer feel. Grips usually range between four and four and five-eighths inches in diameter, so any increase in size is small, but it can be a significant factor in playing well. As you can see, this wrap is made of a porous material that acts as an absorbent and keeps the player's hand from slipping. Now, grip wraps wear out faster than the permanent grip, but they're not as expensive, and wraps can be easily replaced when they become too worn."

Stacy closely examines the wrap and sees that the grip is both bigger and softer than those of other racquets hanging on the wall. She also notices that the grip is slightly larger at its end. "Is there an extra layer of wrap at the end of the grip?" she asks.

"No, that end of the grip is called the butt of the racquet. There's usually a plastic plug in the butt to keep a player's hand from slipping. You see, the butt enlarges that area of the grip where a player rests the pad of her hand."

Stacy looks back at the racquets hanging on the wall and notices that some racquets look longer than others, and some definitely have larger heads than others.

"Racquets normally range in length from twenty-seven inches to twenty-nine inches, although there are a few made longer," Red explains, noticing her study of the racquets. "The difference in length has several effects. Obviously, if a racquet is longer, it gives the player a greater reach. A ball that might have been missed with a shorter racquet can be reached and played with a longer one."

"Then why not have a racquet that's forty inches long?" Stacy wants to know.

"Control," Red declares. "Like most things in racquet design, there is a trade-off. The longer the racquet, the more difficult it is to control.

"There's a similar trade-off in head size," Red continues. "In the old days wooden racquet heads measured in the low 80s. Today, racquet heads usually range from 95 to 115 inches."

"Inches?" Stacy asks, looking at the racquet head and wondering what sort of measurement this could be.

"I'm sorry," Red says. "Racquet heads are measured in square inches of head size. An old wooden racquet head measuring 80 inches had 80 square inches of head size, and a new racquet measuring 110 inches is 110 square inches of head size."

"I understand the advantages of a bigger head," she acknowledges. "Goodness knows, I need all the hitting area I can get. What are the disadvantages?"

"Again, the trade-off is control," Red goes on. "A larger head has more effective hitting area but also greater room for error. If you don't hit the ball in the sweet spot or make a good stroke, it doesn't matter how large your racquet head is, you won't hit the kind of shot you want."

"The what spot?" Stacy asks.

"The SWEET SPOT. That's the area on the racquet, usually in the center, where the ball springs off the racquet cleaner and truer and with better feel. It's like hitting a baseball in the center of the bat. There's a solid feel when that happens, and players call that area the sweet spot."

Stacy writes this down. "You said the sweet spot was usually in the center. Not always?"

"No, not always." Red again reaches up and removes two other racquets from the wall. He lays all three racquets on the table where Stacy can examine them. "Remember, racquets are designed to perform certain ways in order to appeal to the preferences of different players." He shows her three different head designs: an ELLIPTICAL (or oval) head design, with the sweet spot right in the middle; a TEARDROP head design; and a more squared head— the sweet spot on the latter two conforming to the head shape of the racquet.

Stacy can't help wondering if all this racquet info is really important for a complete novice like her.

HEAD SHAPE

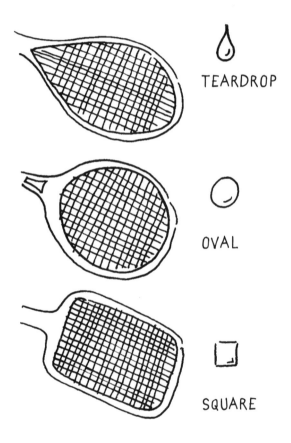

TEARDROP

OVAL

SQUARE

HEAD DESIGN MAKES THE
SWEET SPOT SWEETER

"It's good for you to know this information, because different players have a different feel for racquets," Red adds. "By understanding the basics of racquet design, you have a better understanding of why one racquet feels better than another. You have choices to make as a beginner. It's better to be informed.

"Furthermore, design alone isn't the only factor in determining how a racquet feels or how it plays. Another factor to consider is the STIFFNESS of the racquet frame. This is a measurement of how much resistance or flex the racquet frame has."

"And that's important?" Stacy presses.

"Oh, very," Red explains. "A flexible racquet will have more whip, which is great if you're trying to play soft, finesse tennis. The downside, again, is control. The more whip there is in a racquet, the less control you have."

"So, I need to get a racquet with a stiff frame."

"Yes, I recommend everyone start out with a racquet on the stiff side and simply adjust string tension to suit your particular game."

Stacy looks up from her notes. "String tension? You mean there's another variable I need to remember?"

"Yes, indeed," Red confirms. "STRING TENSION is an important variable to decide on. Make sure your racquet has a moderate string tension, not too stiff and not too flexible. Starting out middle-of-the-road is a good rule to follow in racquet selection and string tension."

Once again Red reaches into the inventory of racquets, only this time he retrieves one that is fully strung. He holds the racquet out so that Stacy can get a good look.

"As you can see, racquets have a set of strings that interlace throughout the FACE of the racquet. The vertical strings, those running lengthwise with the racquet, are called the MAIN STRINGS. The horizontal strings, those running perpendicular to the shaft, are called the cross strings. These particular strings are constructed from a manmade blend of Kevlar and other multifiber synthetics or nylon, but some strings are still made from GUT.

"Gut?" Stacy inquires, unsure if she really wants to hear this explanation.

"Yes, almost all natural strings are actually made from cow intestines with a low percentage made from sheep intestines. They are woven into a natural string that's used by many of the best players in the world."

Stacy straightens her back a little. "Look, I'm not an animal rights fanatic or anything, but I can assure you I don't want that."

"I can assure you, you don't need it," Red says. "Natural gut strings do provide better feel for the top-level players; but until you reach almost-world-class status, you can't tell the difference between gut and synthetic strings. Gut is more expensive, and because it's a natural fiber, it is more susceptible to elements such as moisture, heat, and cold. Gut also breaks more easily because of friction. That's why you see all the top players on television carrying so many different racquets and examining their strings so frequently. They're checking for wear. An interesting thing to look for in televised tennis is when a player adds string-a-lings.

"Dingalings?" Stacy queries.

"No," Red laughs heartily. "STRING-A-LINGS. Many times between points in a match or between games, you will see tennis pros take small devices that look like letter openers and work them in between the main and cross strings of their racquets. What they're doing is adding string-a-lings, small plastic dividers that keep the main and cross strings from rubbing against each other. This cuts down on breakage due to friction.

"Of course, that's not the only quirk great players have. Ivan Lendl changed racquets every nine games or every ball change regardless of the circumstances. Michael Chang restrings all his racquets before every match whether or not he's used them. He feels the usable life span of his gut strings is one day. That's an extreme case, and Chang spends more than fifty thousand dollars a year on string. The point is, gut has better feel for better players, but it is more fragile and susceptible to the elements than synthetic string."

After a couple of seconds, Stacy realizes her jaw is hanging open. "I thought you said this was an inexpensive game."

"When you're ranked among the top five in the world, every little thing can mean thousands or even millions of dollars to you," Red explains. "You pay a little more attention and spend a little more money when that's the case."

"So what about this flex thing? What does that mean?" she questions.

Red motions her over to his worktable and points to the machine that looks like some sort of medieval torture device. "This is a stringing machine," Red says. "When stringing a racquet, I have to know how many pounds of pressure the player wants in his or her strings. String tension is a measure of the pounds of pressure applied when stringing the racquet, which, in turn, controls the stiffness or flexibility of the strings.

"By setting the pressure here," he continues, pointing to a lever protruding from one side of the machine, "I can adjust the tension in a racquet's strings anywhere from, say, forty pounds up to over eighty pounds."

"Why's that?" Stacy probes.

Red rubs his chin and considers his answer before speaking. "When a racquet is loosely strung, there is obviously a lot of give, which means shots are cushioned. The shots feel great because everything feels like a sweet spot. The problem is you get a trampoline effect. The ball rockets off the strings with little or no control.

"Now, the opposite is true of strings that are too tight. You have great control, but because of the stiffness of the strings, there's very little feel. The sweet spot is diminished, and it's very difficult to hit any finesse shots. The racquet is like a board."

"What's right for me?" Stacy inquires.

THE STRINGS

STRING TENSION MEANS A LOT WHEN IT COMES TO PICKING THE RIGHT RACQUET.

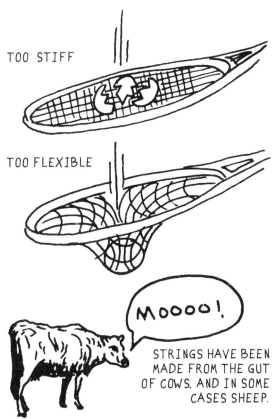

TOO STIFF

TOO FLEXIBLE

MOOOO!

STRINGS HAVE BEEN MADE FROM THE GUT OF COWS, AND IN SOME CASES SHEEP.

MODERN STRINGS ARE MANMADE SYNTHETIC NYLON MONOFILAMENT OR MULTIFILAMENT.

"I don't know," Red declares in a very matter-of-fact tone. "I don't mean that to sound like a cop-out, but no one can tell you what string tension you need without first seeing you hit a ball or at least without talking with you about your objectives. John McEnroe, one of the greatest players, strung his racquet at between forty and fifty pounds. That's pounds of pressure—not very much when you consider John's caliber of play. Bjorn Borg used to string his racquets with eighty pounds of pressure. That's high, but that suited his style of play. Again, as a beginner, you need to stay middle-of-the road. Until you develop a style of play that demands otherwise, I recommend that you don't deviate from the racquet manufacturer's suggested pounds of pressure."

"Okay, so I need to try out racquets before deciding what to buy," Stacy affirms. "Where do I do this? The only racquets I've ever seen, other than in here today, have been when I accidentally wandered into the sporting goods store at the mall."

Red holds up a hand and tells Stacy not to worry. He explains how most tennis clubs and a great number of off-court tennis shops will allow players to try out demonstrator racquets. He suggests to Stacy that she take at least three demo racquets out to the courts. "Ask a pro to help. Remember, the most important point in buying a racquet is your feel and comfort. If it doesn't feel good in your hands, it's not right for you."

Red then notes: "Don't let all this information overwhelm you. The most important thing is to pick equipment that suits your personal needs."

"Good advice," Stacy says.

Red's attention is distracted by a group of ladies entering the shop. Stacy looks over her shoulder and sees that more league players, all in matching skirts and tops, have finished their matches and are crowding inside to discuss their relative fortunes.

"Thanks for all your help, Red. I guess I should be going," she says.

"Nonsense," Red retorts. "You're just getting started."

He raises his hand and gets the attention of one of the league players. "Monique, can I see you for a minute?" he inquires.

A tall, athletic woman with long black hair and a perky smile steps out of the crowd and walks over to Red and Stacy. "Hi, Red."

"Monique Teles, I'd like for you to meet Stacy, our student *du jour*. Stacy and I have been discussing some of the basics of buying a racquet, but I've got to do a restring for Mr. Connors before his afternoon match. Would you mind spending some time with Stacy? She needs to see some of the other things we carry in the shop."

"Sure thing," Monique agrees, politely beckoning with a wave of her hand for Stacy to follow her. "Come with me, Stacy. If there's one thing I know, it's how to shop."

THE RACQUET

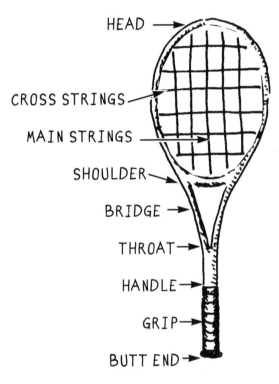

HEAD →

CROSS STRINGS

MAIN STRINGS

SHOULDER →

BRIDGE →

THROAT →

HANDLE →

GRIP →

BUTT END →

18TH CENTURY

WOOD

ALUMINUM

COMPOSITE

FOUR

DRESSED TO MATCH

Stacy follows Monique to an area of the pro shop remarkably similar to the clothing section of a department store. Tastefully appointed wooden fixtures house numerous displays of shirts, shorts, skirts, and shoes, along with more framed action pictures of players Stacy assumes are some of the world's best. Monique maneuvers between two freestanding clothing racks and leads Stacy to a remote corner where a number of cylinders that look like the potato chip cans Stacy normally buys are stacked in a pyramid. "I take it you don't know much about tennis balls," Monique says.

"I know less than not much," Stacy concedes. "I suppose those canisters have balls in them?"

Monique nods. "Tennis balls come in pressurized cans to ensure quality and liveliness." Stacy is surprised by the pop the can makes when Monique opens it.

"Do they always make that sound?" she exclaims.

"If they're properly sealed, yes. It's sort of like listening for the fizz when you open a can of soda."

Stacy retrieves her now well-worn notepad. "I'm sure having new tennis balls isn't a big deal for me. How important can it be?"

"Very important," Monique insists. "It's very tempting for a beginner to use old or used tennis balls, but that's the worst thing you can do. Tennis balls wear out, lose their resiliency, become worn, and perform poorly. Using them is more of a detriment than a benefit."

She goes on to explain that tennis balls are designed to behave with certain characteristics, and while some are more lively than others, as a rule, new tennis balls will rebound between fifty-three and fifty-eight inches when dropped onto a concrete base from a height of one hundred inches.

"You don't want to practice with balls that react differently from the standard. Also, by rule, tennis balls must be white or yellow and between two and one-half and two and five-eighths inches in diameter. The primary reason for that variation in size is the nap of the ball. In the beginning of the sport, tennis balls were simply hollow rubber spheres until an innovator named John Heathcote covered the rubber with two strips of flannel and launched the era of the modern tennis ball. Today, tennis balls can either have a thick nap or one with a relatively smooth surface. A thick nap will make the ball rebound more slowly off the court, while a thin one will allow it to skid or rebound faster."

Continuing her minilecture on balls, Monique says that balls can also be pressurized, which means that the internal air pressure is greater than the external air pressure, much like inflatable basketballs or volleyballs. Pressurization varies in tennis balls, making some balls more lively than others. Also, altitude can have a dramatic effect on the liveliness and pressure of tennis balls, since air is thinner at higher altitudes and balls naturally fly farther. Balls with low pressurization are usually used in high altitudes and are called high-altitude balls.

"If I'm buying new balls, how many do I need?" Stacy asks.

"Well, you only play with one ball at a time, but in the interest of time you should always take a minimum of three balls with you to the court. Of course, if you're practicing, you might need to take an entire BASKET of balls. I suggest you keep an inventory of thirty or more tennis balls around, just in case you find you have a few free hours to go work on your serve."

Stacy doesn't know what a serve is, but she decides to defer that question. "Okay, I can carry three balls around in a can, but how in the world would I get anywhere with thirty or more tennis balls?" she asks.

"Great question," Monique declares. "It's time to accessorize."

Monique leads Stacy over to an area of the shop where a variety of bags, tubes, sunglasses, and other items are displayed around a counter. "One of the first accessory items you want to buy is a bag to carry your racquets and other equipment," Monique announces.

"Racquets?" Stacy queries. "Did you say racquets, as in more than one?"

"Yes. It makes life a lot easier if you have a back-up racquet nearby during a match. What if you break a string during the middle of a game? Without an extra racquet, the entire match stops." She then describes two types of bags Stacy could consider buying:

- a THERMAL RACQUET BAG can hold between one and six racquets. Usually padded, it has full-length shoulder straps for easy carrying around and offers protection from the normal bumps everywhere from the living room to the trunk of the car. Usually, these racquet bags have enough room for a few balls and some other sundries.
- an EQUIPMENT BAG, sometimes called a TOURNAMENT CARRYALL or a PRO BAG. This is a lightweight but durable athletic bag that's large enough to carry all the equipment, a change of clothes, balls, and even a boxed lunch.

Stacy makes note of the differences between the two bags.

"As for your question about balls," Monique continues, "if you really decide you're going to spend a lot of time practicing and you need to transport a great number of balls to and from the court, I suggest you look into one of two options."

Monique picks up a plastic cylinder that looks like a cross between a mailing tube from the post office and a fly rod case. "You can buy a PICK-UP TUBE, or BALL RETRIEVER, as it's sometimes called." She holds up the tube and Stacy sees that the device has a capturing mechanism on one end and is open on the other. "These tubes can hold between fifteen and twenty balls. Not only do they neatly store your practice balls, they keep you from having to bend over, which after several hours of practice is a really big deal.

"If you become ambitious, you can buy a PRACTICE BASKET, or BALL CADDIE, as it's also known. This is nothing more than a plastic woven basket, with gaps between the bottom weaves large enough so you can force a ball through the openings without having to bend over. These baskets can hold up to thirty or more balls, but they are usually reserved for teaching professionals or the diehard player who practices for hours on end. In most cases, a pick-up tube will suit your needs. Next up, we want to make sure you're properly outfitted."

"That sounds like it could be dangerous to my credit card," Stacy observes.

Monique laughs and leads Stacy back to the clothing displays. "Let's start from the bottom up," she announces. "Do you own proper tennis shoes?"

"What do you mean by 'proper'?"

Monique glances down at the sneakers Stacy has worn almost every day since their arrival in town. They are worn and flat with plain canvas uppers and little visible support. But as Stacy will quickly tell anyone who asks, these are the most comfortable shoes she's ever owned. Monique tells her what she already knows: As comfortable as they may be, the shoes she is wearing are not right for tennis.

"Fortunately, you don't need to take out a second mortgage to get a good pair of tennis shoes," Monique reassures her, before going on to explain some key points to remember when shopping for shoes:

- Tennis requires a great deal of stopping and starting, so support is critical. Pick a shoe that has great arch support and good lateral support.
- Make sure the heel support of the shoe is sturdy but soft. You can't play for very long in a shoe that rubs blisters on your feet, and you can't play at all if you strain an Achilles tendon.
- Make sure the soles of the shoes are appropriate for a variety of surfaces. Very few of us have the luxury of owning a pair of shoes for each type of surface we encounter, like the pros do. The best thing to do is to pick a supportive tennis shoe. High-top basketball or running shoes are out as a rule.
- Most importantly, pick shoes that are comfortable.

Stacy recalls the old photo of William Renshaw. She mentions to Monique that in the picture William appeared to be wearing street shoes.

"That's not far from accurate," Monique replies. "Back in the old days, anything with a rubber sole could be considered a tennis shoe. Some players actually wore spiked shoes to keep their footing on the grass, but, hey, men also wore slacks and ties and women wore long dresses. Comfort and mobility weren't high priorities back then."

"Which brings up our next point, I guess," Stacy says. "Now that I have the shoes, what should I wear? I don't want to be inappropriate, but I don't want to dress like I'm going to Wimbledon either."

Monique motions Stacy over to a rack of skirts that Stacy's mother would have described as "skimpy."

"Wow, those take miniskirts to a new level," Stacy pronounces.

Monique tells Stacy that the evolutionary pendulum of tennis attire has gone full swing. Today comfort and mobility are foremost. Fortunately, designers, starting with the famous (and at one time infamous) Ted Tinling, have paired style with comfort and made today's tennis attire as attractive as it is functional.

"You can be as stylish or as casual as your personal tastes dictate," Monique tells her. "And, oh, by the way, if you did want to dress like you were going to Wimbledon, you'd pick white. The All England Club has an all-white rule governing tennis attire. White used to be the norm to play tennis in until all the members of the U.S. Davis Cup team showed up one year in yellow shirts at the U.S. Open. The Open became more 'enlightened' that day.

"Anyway, a stylish skirt, a matching top, and some BLOOMERS, and you'll be on your way."

THE SHOES

GET THE RIGHT SHOES FOR
THE RIGHT GAME.

IF YOU'RE BUYING ONLY ONE PAIR,
BUY A GOOD TENNIS SHOE.

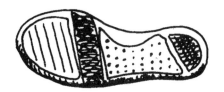

SUPPORT MAKES A DIFFERENCE.

INSOLE FOR
ARCH SUPPORT

FOOTFRAME FOR
TIGHT FIT

RUBBER SOLE FOR
DURABILITY

"Bloomers?" Stacy echoes.

"Yes, bloomers, tennis panties," Monique declares. "You didn't think you wore that miniskirt with nothing under it, did you?"

Stacy smiles and shakes her head. "Okay, assume I've bought my shoes, my comfortable clothes, bloomers included, and all my equipment. Do I need anything else?"

"Just a few things," Monique replies, and Stacy gets her pen ready once more. Monique's list includes:

- Tennis socks, which have greater comfort and absorption, are more durable and provide better cushion than other athletic socks.
- Absorbent, elastic wristbands or sweatbands, which not only keep perspiration from running onto the hands and affecting grip but also provide a convenient sweat rag to wipe eyes and hands.
- A hat with some form of absorbent liner or a headband to keep perspiration off the face and to keep the sun out of the eyes.
- Sunscreen and other items that one would normally use in any outdoor activity.

Stacy writes down all the items on the list. When she looks back up from her notes, she sees another woman, dressed exactly like Monique, standing next to her.

"This is our league director, Betty Jean Prince," Monique says. "Stacy is a student here today, Betty. She came here knowing nothing—"

"Absolutely nothing about tennis," Stacy sheepishly interrupts, completing the thought.

CLOTHES

GET THE RIGHT CLOTHES FOR
THE RIGHT GAME.

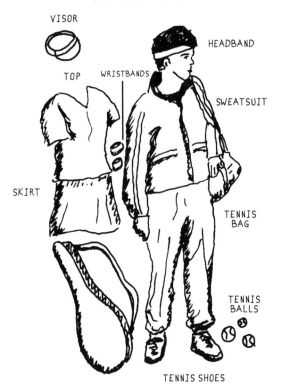

VISOR

HEADBAND

TOP WRISTBANDS

SWEATSUIT

SKIRT

TENNIS
BAG

TENNIS
BALLS

TENNIS SHOES

IN THE PAST, WOMEN
WORE FULL-LENGTH
DRESSES AND MEN
WORE SUITS

Betty's face breaks into a huge smile. "Well, how wonderful. Let me welcome you to this great game. Oh, by the way, these are league uniforms we're wearing. We just finished playing DOUBLES."

Stacy's blank expression poses the next question for her: What are doubles?

Sensing Stacy's frustration, Monique suggests, "Betty, would you have some time to give her an overview on how tennis is played?" Then, turning back to Stacy, she inquires, "I hope that's not too presumptuous. Do you know how to play, or keep score, or any of those things?"

Stacy smiles and shakes her head.

Betty reassures her, "I'm no expert, but I'll be happy to share what I can. Let's go talk things over at lunch, Stacy."

FIVE

COURT IS IN SESSION

Betty orders fruit salad and bottled water, and Stacy picks the highly recommended turkey sandwich. While they wait for their lunches, Betty draws Stacy out with some simple questions. After a few minutes of chitchat, Betty hears the story of Matt's office tournament and Stacy's thirty-day deadline.

"Learning the game well enough to play in a company tournament shouldn't be too difficult," Betty says.

Stacy shakes her head. "I don't know." She holds up her almost full notepad. "I've learned a lot already, but I still don't know anything about courts or how the game is played."

Betty reassures Stacy: "Don't worry. Once you get into it, you'll find tennis to be fun, fast, and easy to learn."

The food arrives, and Stacy's sandwich is good. After asking the waitress for another glass of water, she turns her attention back to the questions at hand. "Both Red and Monique tell me I need to test equipment on a court before I buy. Unfortunately, I don't know enough about courts to make any intelligent choices, which puts me right back at square one."

Betty finishes a bite of her salad before answering. "Red and Monique are right. Also, you need to be aware of the kind of surface you're playing—"

Stacy interrupts, "I don't know what you mean by 'surface.'"

Betty nods and explains the three basic types of court surfaces and their playing characteristics:

- Since the original tennis courts were modified croquet lawns, grass was the first accepted playing surface. It's a very fast surface, meaning the tennis ball bounces or actually skids off the surface quickly.

- CLAY courts (packed clay surfaces) are much slower. The style of play and the type of player who excels on clay differs from those on other surfaces.

- The third type of surfaces are known as hard courts, or hard surfaces. These courts encompass a number of different materials ranging from asphalt and concrete to complex synthetics. Hard courts have become the most common and popular surfaces because they require very little maintenance and they offer the most balanced medium between fast, skidding grass courts and slower, rougher clay courts. Also, manufacturers of synthetic materials can control the speed of hard courts by changing the texture of the surface.

Occasionally, one still finds a wooden court outdoors and some carpeted surfaces indoors.

Stacy writes all this in her notepad, but she feels that Betty doesn't fully appreciate the depth of her ignorance. "Betty, I assume all those lines on the court mean something. I also assume where you stand on the court is important. Whether I'm on grass, clay, carpet, or rubber, I might as well be stuck in quicksand if I don't know what to do."

Betty laughs at this, but nods in understanding. "All courts have the same dimensions. Playing conditions might be different and each opponent you face will present a new and different challenge, but the court configuration, the rules, and the scoring remain constant no matter where you go.

"It's interesting how tennis courts evolved over the years," Betty adds. "Back in the early days, they were shaped like an hourglass, nine feet narrower at the net than at the two baselines."

"How did it change?" Stacy probes.

"Major Wingfield's rules called for the court to be sixty feet long and for the net to be four feet, eight inches high at all points. It's not clear what the logic was behind those dimensions, but it's commonly assumed that the croquet lawns set aside for tennis lent themselves to those quirky measurements. Of course, different places had different rules and different courts. It wasn't until the All England Club in Wimbledon established what they deemed the universal rules of tennis that courts became standardized. The Wimbledon committee settled on a rectangular court that is seventy-eight feet long and twenty-seven feet wide for singles play. It's wider for doubles, which we'll get to in a minute. Also, the net height went through several changes along the way, but by the early 1880s the net was established at its present height of three feet, six inches at the sides, drooping to three feet in the middle. That's where it's been for over a hundred years, and there are no plans to change it.

Stacy draws a rectangle and bisects it with several scratchy lines to represent a net. She then marks all the dimensions but realizes there are still some important parts missing. "What about all those lines in the middle?" she inquires.

Betty explains that all lines on a court have distinct functions. She takes a great deal of time showing Stacy how the court is laid out and what each area means.

- The exterior lines of the court are called BASE-LINES and SIDELINES. However, there are two different sets of sidelines: the SINGLES SIDELINES that set the singles court width at twenty-seven feet, and the DOUBLES SIDELINES that add an additional four and a half feet to each side of the court, making the doubles court thirty-six feet wide.
- The lane or alley between the singles sideline and doubles sideline is called the DOUBLES ALLEY.

- The posts that hold up the net on each end are, appropriately, called NET POSTS. In order to keep the net a consistent height, there are also SINGLES STICKS, which are added three feet outside the singles court during singles play, thus boosting the net to the same height as the DOUBLES POSTS.

"Okay," Stacy jumps in, holding up her hand. "What are doubles and singles?"

"In a singles match one person plays another, one-on-one," Betty replies.

"That makes sense," Stacy observes. "So, following that logic, I assume a doubles match is two-on-two?"

Betty nods. "That's right. Two partners play against two other partners in doubles. Since there are four people on the court instead of two, the doubles court is wider."

She goes on to describe how, within the baselines and sidelines, the court is divided even further:

- On both sides of the net, the court is divided into smaller SERVICE COURTS, each court being twenty-one feet long and thirteen and a half feet wide. These are called left service court and right service court, the direction being the perspective of a player standing on the baseline.

- The line that designates the twenty-one-foot mark for the service courts is called the service line, and the line that bisects the left and right service courts is called the CENTERLINE.

- The remaining eighteen feet of the court from the service line to the baseline is called the BACKCOURT, or NO-MAN'S-LAND.

- A small hashmark at the center on the base line is called the CENTERMARK.

"What does all that mean?" Stacy blurts out in frustration. "Service court, centermark, backcourt, no-man's-land. . . . It sounds like a mix between a computer program and a John Wayne movie."

Betty laughs. "The best way to learn what all this means is to actually walk through the playing of a match. Once you understand the basics of how the game is played, all the things you've learned so far will fall into place."

"Then by all means walk me through it," Stacy exclaims.

THE COURT

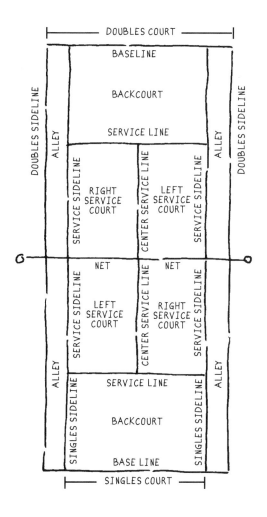

Six

Game, Set, Match (and More)

"First, you have to determine who starts the game and which side of the court each player will take," Betty begins. "This is usually done by either spinning the racquet and calling which side will be up or down, or by flipping a coin. The winner of the coin toss can either choose to serve (start the game) or receive, or she can choose which side of the court she prefers, or she can defer and let the other player make the choice. If the coin-toss winner chooses to serve first, the other player picks which side of the court she wants to defend."

"But, what does 'serve' mean?" Stacy asks.

"The serve is the first stroke. It's when the ball is put into play and the point begins," Betty explains.

"Got it," Stacy affirms while writing. "I win, so I get to either start the game, receive serve, choose the side, or defer and let my opponent choose."

"Correct. Let's say it's a calm day, no wind, and sunlight isn't a problem, so the end of the court you're on isn't a big deal."

"Then I would choose whether or not to serve," Stacy states.

"You would choose to either serve or RECEIVE," Betty declares. "Now, the strategy of serving or receiving is very important, depending on how you play. If you need a little more time to warm up or you don't feel comfortable starting a match by serving, you will want to receive first and try to break your opponent's serve early."

Stacy talks as she writes, "So, I either serve or try to break up the serve—"

"No, it's BREAK SERVE," Betty interrupts. "That's when you win a game while your opponent is serving. You will also hear it referred to as a SERVICE BREAK or just BREAK. It's important that you break your opponent's serve and that you keep your opponent from breaking yours. It's sort of an unwritten expectation in tennis to hold your serve. For good players, it's almost expected. If you do that, you win. A lot of people want to serve first because they feel they can win their serve, or HOLD SERVE, and therefore always be up by one game.

"The serve is the first stroke of a point, and it always begins from behind the baseline. The server stands on the right side of the court behind the baseline in an area between the right sideline and the centermark. You then toss the ball into the air with your free hand and strike it with your racquet before it hits the ground. Of course, you aren't just trying to hit it, you're trying to hit it into a certain area. The ball must cross over the net before bouncing and land in your opponent's right service court—that's the service court diagonally opposite from you."

Stacy looks up with another confused stare. "I'm on the right side of the court, and I'm hitting into her right court—"

"Yes, but remember, she's facing you. Her right is your left; therefore, her right service court is diagonally opposite from your right."

Stacy smiles and nods. The light bulb just went on.

"You get two tries to serve the ball into your opponent's service court. If you miss the service court on your first try, it's called a FAULT. If you don't get the ball over the net on your first try, that's also a fault. If your foot crosses the baseline or encroaches beyond the centermark, it's also a fault, but it's called a FOOT FAULT.

"When the ball strikes the net cord on top of the net on the serve, the net judge calls 'Net.' Then the umpire calls 'Let' if the ball landed in and 'Fault' if the ball was out. If you hit the top of the net during a rally, it's called a 'net cord.' A common mistake is the use of the term NET CORD. That's the tape you find along the top of the net. It's a 'net cord' during a rally, but if you hit it on your serve, it's called a 'let.' Got it?"

"I think so," Stacy sighs. "If I miss with my first serve, it's called a fault, and I get another chance. What if I miss again?"

"That's called a DOUBLE FAULT, and you lose the point," Betty says.

"If I lose the point, does my opponent then get to serve?"

"No. Unlike racquetball and some other racquet sports where service is changed every time the server loses a point, tennis is structured where one player retains service for an entire game," Betty points out. "However, after each point, you change the service court. For example, you start the game behind your right service court serving to your opponent's right service court; but after the first point, you move left of the centermark and serve to your opponent's left service court. After the second point, you move back to the right side, and on and on until the game is complete. Your opponent then serves the entire second game under the same procedures."

Stacy reads through her notes to make sure she understands what Betty has outlined. "Okay, the server has to stand behind the baseline, somewhere between the plane of the sideline and the centermark. Where does the person receiving the serve stand?"

"Anywhere she wants," Betty replies. "Obviously, if the ball is being served to your right service court, it just makes sense that you stand somewhere behind that area, but there are no restrictions.

"The object of the game is to hit the ball where your opponent is not, or to force an ERROR. As long as you hit the ball over the net and into the court, you can do it from almost anywhere. The only thing you cannot do when receiving a serve is hit the ball before it hits the ground. A served ball has to hit the ground before it can be returned, although on subsequent shots you can hit the ball before it bounces. When you hit a return shot before the ball hits the ground, the shot is called a VOLLEY. SERVE-AND-VOLLEY is an aggressive style of play that many players prefer. By charging the net and hitting a volley, serve-and-volley players often hit quick winners."

"Hitting the ball out of the air is called VOLLEY-ING, like volleyball?" Stacy asks.

"That's right," Betty says. "That's an important term to know, because it's very misused. Many people assume anytime you're hitting the ball back and forth over the net, you and your opponent are volleying. That's wrong, and nothing tips good players off to your inexperience quicker than misusing that word. When you're hitting shots back and forth you are RALLYING; when the ball doesn't hit the ground, you are volleying."

Betty goes on to say that at the end of each odd-numbered game (such as one, three, five), the players switch ends of the court; therefore, if sun, wind, or other elements are factors, both players will be subjected to the same conditions. She also explains that tennis matches can be broken down into several segments:

- Each time the ball is put into play, it's considered a POINT. Each player is trying to win each individual point.

- A series of points make up a game. Win enough points and you win the game.
- A series of games make up a SET.
- A predetermined number of sets make up a match.

"Usually, matches are a best two-out-of-three sets, although some tournaments have best three-out-of-five set matches," Betty notes. "The set winner is the first person to win six games, but you must win a set by two games. If you win six games and your opponent wins only two, three, or four games, you win the set. If you win two sets, you win the match."

"What if you don't win by two games? I mean, if my opponent and I both win all the games when we're serving, we could go on forever and never win by two games."

"That's one of the reasons I stressed the importance of breaking your opponent's serve and HOLD-ING SERVE," Betty explains. "Back to your original question: There was a time in tennis when the scenario you're describing was not only possible but common. Matches went on for hours. In fact, the 1967 Newport Invitational holds the record for the longest professional match. One doubles set went to forty-nine games and another went to twenty-two games. Then a tennis innovator named Jimmy Van Alen devised a tiebreaking system called the nine-point, sudden-death TIEBREAK. Under Van Alen's system, when a set reaches a 6-6 tie the players enter a tiebreak, and the first player to reach five points

POINTS MAKE GAMES,
GAMES MAKE SETS, AND
SETS MAKE MATCHES.

A POINT BEGINS WHEN A
SERVER SERVES.

VOLLEYS DON'T
HIT THE GROUND;
RALLIES OFTEN DO.

wins. The player who would have normally served the thirteenth game serves for two points, then her opponent serves the next two points; the original server serves the next two, and the opponent serves the last three points, if necessary. Also, every four points of the tiebreak, the players CHANGE SIDES."

"So, in a sudden-death tiebreak, the serve alternates, and you don't have to win by two?" Stacy asks as she reviews her notes.

"That's true," Betty affirms. "But let me also tell you that there is another tiebreak system started and used by the ITF. It is known as the LINGERING DEATH tiebreak, which is commonly called the 'twelve-point tiebreak.' The first player serves one point, the opponent then serves two points, and on and on it goes. In this tiebreak, players switch sides every six points. Lingering death stipulates that the winner is the first player who reaches seven points, provided she wins by a margin of two. Theoretically, this could also go on forever; but, for the most part, this tiebreak system works well."

It occurs to Stacy that tennis is a much longer, more complicated game than she had thought. "The games must be short," she comments. "I mean, there are so many of them. Are games like the tiebreaks, the first player to serve five or so wins?"

"Not exactly," Betty concedes. "Tennis has a unique system of scoring. Your score in tennis is either LOVE, FIFTEEN, THIRTY, FORTY, advantage, or game."

"Forty! You mean each game goes to forty? There's nothing to love about that," Stacy exclaims.

Betty laughs. Then she tells Stacy that there are not forty points in a game, and she goes over the strange way that points are counted:

- Love in tennis means zero. The term comes from the French word *l'oeuf,* which means "egg," implying goose egg or zero.
- The first point of a game is fifteen.
- The second point of a game is thirty, which would imply that each point counts as fifteen, except the third point is forty.
- The last point is simply game; however, you must win a game by two points.
- If a game becomes tied at forty, the proper tennis term is DEUCE, because it's impossible for the next point to decide the winner.
- The next point scored after deuce is called AD-VANTAGE, or simply AD. If the player with the advantage wins the next point, the game is over. If the advantage player loses the next point, the score goes back to deuce. This process continues until one player wins by two points.

"So," Betty reviews, "the points in a tennis game are love, fifteen, thirty, forty, deuce, advantage, and game. No one knows the exact origins of the scoring system, and even though historians have been studying the game for years, no one even knows where the word *tennis* came from. However, as the scoring goes, once you understand deuce and advantage, you no longer need to worry about which service court is the right and which is the left. The right service court for both players is always the DEUCE COURT, and the left service court is always the AD COURT. Rather than referring to the service courts as right and left service courts, most experienced players simply call them the deuce and ad courts."

"Sort of like port and starboard when you're boating," Stacy offers.

Betty nods. "I never thought of that analogy, but you're right. It prevents you from worrying about whose right and whose left you're considering."

Stacy reviews all her notes, and Betty senses that the information is overwhelming. "Let's take a little quiz," she offers. "You are serving to your opponent in game one of your first set, and you win the first two points. What's the score?"

Stacy considers the scenario. "Love-thirty," she answers.

"Close," Betty says. "It's thirty-love. When calling out the score, you always call the server's score first. That way there's no confusion."

Betty continues, "You win the first three points, but your opponent comes back and wins the next three points. What's the score?"

Stacy walks through the game in her mind before answering, "Deuce."

"Right. Very good!" Betty exclaims. "I think you've got it."

Stacy isn't so sure, but she does feel more comfortable. "Now that I know *what* to do, how do I learn *how* to do it?" she asks.

THE SCORE

 LOVE - 0

 FIFTEEN - FIRST POINT

 THIRTY - SECOND POINT

 FORTY - THIRD POINT

 DEUCE - TIED AT FORTY

 ADVANTAGE - NEXT POINT AFTER DEUCE

 GAME - WINNER

"You take lessons, of course," Betty responds. "Don't worry. Come with me. There's someone here I'd like for you to meet."

They leave the club restaurant and walk outside along a nicely landscaped path. Two women and two men stroll past them, obviously on their way to a match. As they pass the first set of courts, Stacy looks closely at the surface.

"Is that clay?" she asks.

Betty is pleasantly surprised by the question. "Yes, it is," she says. "My, you are a quick learner. We have both clay and hard courts here at Saddle Ridge."

They approach a large fence protecting one of the courts, and Betty opens the nearby door. On the court a trim, athletic man in white shorts and shirt is wiping his forehead with a towel. Betty walks ahead and waves to the man. "Hi, Arthur," she calls. "How was your practice?"

"Still having some trouble with my crosscourt backhand," he replies. "But I'm getting there." The man has walked over to the edge of the court and is now standing in front of Stacy. He pitches the towel aside and extends a firm right hand. "Hello, I'm Arthur Smash."

"Arthur, I'd like for you to meet Stacy, Saddle Ridge's star student of the day," Betty says.

Stacy chuckles, somewhat embarrassed by Betty's grand introduction. "I'm afraid Betty is far too kind. I started the day knowing absolutely nothing about tennis."

"And now?" Arthur asks.

"Now, I know a little more than absolutely nothing."

Arthur laughs. "Well, it's a pleasure having you out today, Stacy. I'm sure Betty has taught you well."

"Oh, she has," Stacy answers.

"That's why I wanted Stacy to meet you, Arthur," Betty jumps in. "She's an incredibly quick pupil who has learned about equipment, courts, scoring, and the like, but I'm afraid she hasn't a clue about what to do once we put a racquet in her hands. I'd hoped you could spend a few minutes priming her on the basics of learning the game."

Arthur looks at his watch. "Tell you what," he says. "I have a lesson in an hour, and I don't have anything to do between now and then." He looks down at Stacy's wonderfully comfortable but totally inadequate shoes. "I take it you're not looking for a lesson today," he observes.

"Oh, no," she agrees.

"I was thinking more along the lines of a lesson on lessons," Betty interjects. "Stacy needs to know what to expect and how to prepare for her entry into lesson-taking."

"Sounds like a good plan," Arthur comments. "Just let me get my things, and I'll be right back for your lesson on how to take lessons."

"Thank you, Arthur," Betty says. "I must be going. Good luck, Stacy. I hope to see you out here playing soon."

Seven

Baseline Basics

Arthur and Stacy settle on a courtside bench, and Arthur retrieves a bottle of water from his bag while Stacy regards his every move. Sitting down with a drink is, for him, an act performed with grace and efficiency. When he speaks, she is pleased by his soft-spoken and mellow delivery.

"So, you've never taken a tennis lesson, is that right?" he inquires.

"I've never been near a tennis court before today," she admits, then she tells him her dilemma.

Arthur smiles and drinks some water before speaking. "You seem to have caught on quite well. You'll find the benefits of this game far outlast one tournament. You can enjoy tennis socially and competitively for the rest of your life. There are no ability requirements attached to tennis's fun factor. From your first lesson and your first day on the court you can have a great time learning tennis."

"Which brings us to the subject at hand," Stacy states. "How do I take a lesson? What do I do? Where do I go?"

Arthur tells her that most established clubs have certified teaching professionals either on staff or serving as independent contractors. In most cases it isn't necessary to be a member of the club to take lessons from the pro, but restrictions vary with each club. He also advises her that finding the right professional is more important than finding the right club. A good teaching pro will always have a court at his or her disposal.

Stacy retrieves the notepad and writes. "It's important to find a pro, not just somebody who knows tennis, right?"

"Right. While meaning well, most amateurs don't have the training and experience to teach proper technique, strategy, and shot making. You really do yourself a disservice by not going to a certified teaching pro."

Stacy then poses the logical follow-up questions, "How do I know if a pro is certified? Who does the certifying? How do I know if a pro is really qualified?"

"There are two national organizations that certify teaching professionals," Arthur replies. "They are the USPTA, which stands for UNITED STATES PRO-FESSIONAL TENNIS ASSOCIATION, and the USPTR, the UNITED STATES PROFESSIONAL TENNIS REG-ISTRY. Both organizations require their professionals to undergo a series of training programs and tests to become certified teachers. When you're interviewing a tennis pro, make sure he or she is certified by one of these organizations."

"When I'm interviewing a pro," Stacy says in dismay, "I'm the one who knows absolutely nothing about tennis. How am I supposed to interview a tennis pro?"

Arthur pauses before answering. "Choosing a tennis professional is a two-way street. The professional's job is to teach you the basics no matter your skill level, but you have to feel comfortable in your relationship with the pro. You have to relate to what your professional tells you, and your pro has to be cognizant of your ability and your aptitude for learning. In order to gain that comfort level you need to speak to more than one tennis pro." Then he enumerates a number of things to consider:

- First, how convenient and accessible is the pro? If you plan to take lessons regularly, it doesn't do you much good to pick a pro who's on the other side of town or someone who's booked up for the next six months.
- How expensive are the lessons? You're paying for the professional's time and expertise, and depending on where you take your lessons, you could also be paying for court times. As a beginner, you don't want to pick a professional who specializes in coaching touring pros. You also don't want to pick someone just because he or she has a low hourly rate.
- Are you comfortable with the pro you're considering? Be honest about where you are with

YOU WOULDN'T GO TO AN UNLICENSED DOCTOR, SO DON'T GO TO AN UNCERTIFIED PRO.

your game and discuss your goals. A five- or
ten-minute conversation with a pro will give
you a good idea if you and the pro click.

- How much time do you have to practice? You
can't take one lesson and become an expert.
Discuss this with the pro.

"Since you have a pretty good grasp of how the
game is played," Arthur continues, "you can expect
the first series of lessons to be devoted to three tennis fundamentals that remain unchanged no matter
how proficient you become. They are GRIP, STANCE,
and SWING.

"The GRIP, as the name implies, concerns how
you place your hands on the racquet. You can expect
to hear such terms as EASTERN GRIP, WESTERN
GRIP, and CONTINENTAL GRIP."

Stacy looks up from her notes. "I assume you
don't use a different grip for each continent," she
comments.

Arthur laughs. "No, you use different grips for
different types of shots. The names simply refer to
your hand position on the racquet." Arthur opens
his racquet bag and retrieves one of his racquets.
"See how my thumb and index finger form a V
when I grip the racquet? When my hand is positioned so that the V is pointing toward my right
shoulder (for right-handers), that's called an Eastern
grip (think of shaking hands with the racquet).
When the hand is rotated to the right and the V is
pointing well right of your right shoulder, that's
called a Western grip. And when the hand is rotated

to the left, with the V pointing to your left shoulder, that's called a Continental grip. Finally, there's the backhand grip, where the V is pointing to the left of my left shoulder. These different grips are important because you will change your grip when you hit different shots. Your pro will make recommendations on your grip, but by knowing the different ways to grip the racquet, you can be ahead of the game when you show up for your first lesson."

"I notice that white-knuckle death grip wasn't on the list," Stacy comments as she finishes writing. "I'm sure that's the way I'll grip the racquet for a while."

Arthur laughs, then remarks, "You might grip it that way until you hit your first backhand. Then you'll loosen up."

Stacy stares blankly at him. She has no idea what "backhand" means. "I give up," she concedes.

"That's just one of many swings you will learn during your first lesson, but before you make your first contact, you will have to learn the proper stance. Your pro will walk you through different stances." Arthur then covers some things that will always remain constant:

- Always keep your head up so your eyes can see the court and the ball.
- Always stay on the balls of your feet, ready to bound to the next shot.
- Balance is important. If you're off balance, you are out of control, and the likelihood of hitting a good shot, or even making good contact, is nil.

"As to your question about the backhand," Arthur says, "shots other than the serve can be put into one of two categories: Either you are hitting a FOREHAND or a BACKHAND.

"If I were attempting to hit a ball with my hand, the shot I would hit with my palm is called a forehand, and the shot I would hit with the back of my hand is called a backhand. The same principle applies when I'm holding a racquet."

"So a backhand shot is one that's across your body, and a forehand is always a shot from the side where you're holding the racquet," Stacy notes.

"Right," Arthur says. "For a right-handed player, a forehand shot is hit from the right side and a backhand shot is played from the left side, or across the player's body. In the beginning your forehand will probably be stronger than your backhand. That's why a number of players hit what's known as a TWO-HANDED BACKHAND; they actually put both hands on the racquet to hit a backhand."

"That helps?" Stacy inquires.

"Oh, sure," Arthur acknowledges. "Placing both hands on the racquet cuts down on your reach, but it does give you more power. Players with a great amount of foot speed who can cover the court easily might choose to hit a two-handed backhand for added power. It's a matter of preference and style. No matter what you might hear shots called—volleys, drop-volleys, overheads, down-the-lines, crosscourts—they are all either forehands or backhands."

Stacy shakes her head. "I know what a volley is, but what do the rest of those things mean?"

"There are many different shots, and many different swings that affect those shots," Arthur tells her. "Obviously, the objective of tennis is to hit shots that force your opponent to make errors or to get out of position. Sounds easy enough, right?"

"Oh, yeah," Stacy sighs. "I'll be jumping right out on the court and winning game after game with that strategy." Even though she's only known Arthur a few minutes, Stacy feels comfortable joking around with him, and he seems just as eager to join in the levity.

When the laughter dies down, Arthur declares, "It sounds like a simple thing, but it's too often overlooked: No matter how good or bad you're playing, you should always change a losing game."

"What does that mean?" Stacy asks.

Arthur moves his hands and becomes more animated as he explains. "If you are playing a match and your opponent is winning, change something. If you're hitting to your opponent's forehand side and losing points, try hitting to her backhand. If you're losing from the baseline, try coming up to the net for some volleys. The point is, if the type of game you're playing isn't winning, try something else."

Stacy looks up from her notepad with a sheepish grin. "You're right. That should be a simple thing."

"You would be shocked by the number of people who stick with a losing game to the bitter end," Arthur continues. "Of course, in order to change the type of game you're playing, or even to understand what all this means, you have to have a good working knowledge of the different types of shots. When I use the word *stroke,* or *swing,* I am referring to the physical pass made at the ball. The shot is the result, the flight of the ball. The motion that caused it is the swing or stroke.

Arthur then details the five basic types of shots in tennis, each of which has variations depending on where and how it is hit:

- The first shot is the SERVICE, or SERVE, played from behind the baseline.
- The second type of shot is called a GROUND STROKE, which is played from the backcourt or behind the baseline. It's a RETURN once the ball has hit the ground. One shot in a rally is called a groundstroke.
- The opposite of a groundstroke is a VOLLEY. The ball is intercepted and returned before it hits the court. Volleys can be played anytime during a point except on the serve. A volley is hit from closer to the net.
- A shot hit above your head, similar to the service motion, is called an OVERHEAD.
- The fifth type of shot is called a LOB. As the name implies, a lob is a high, lofty shot used to play over the head of someone who has charged the net.

"Sort of a volleyer's 'gotcha'," Stacy interjects.

Arthur laughs, "I've never heard it put quite like that, but you're exactly right. It's a sickening feeling to be standing at the net thinking you've just hit a

THE FIRST THINGS YOU CAN
EXPECT TO LEARN ARE THE GRIP,
THE STANCE, AND THE SWING.

GRIP

STANCE

SWING

winner, only to have your opponent lob a shot over your head, which you know you can't reach."

"Well, I'm sure I'll have my share of sickening feelings out there, with or without any lobs," Stacy concedes. In reviewing her notes, she thinks of another question: "You said these five types of shots have some different variations. What did you mean by that?"

"The five shots I just described—the serve, the groundstroke, the volley, the overhead, the lob— simply refer to the flight of the ball." Arthur then lists some of the different terms for how and where those shots are played:

- PASSING SHOT—a ball hit past one's opponent who is charging toward the net, or who is at the net
- CROSSCOURT SHOT—a ball played diagonally across the court
- DOWN-THE-LINE SHOT—a ball returned down the same sideline from which it was played; tough shot to hit, but it can catch the opponent off guard and hit a winner
- DROP SHOT—another touch-shot that's hard to master but great to use; is hit very softly in an attempt to drop the ball just over the net with very little bounce; if opponent plays behind the baseline, it can catch her off guard.
- CHIP SHOT—another shot to catch opponent off guard; played short, although not as short as the drop shot; usually one that you try to land at opponent's feet when she's at the net, to make it difficult to hit an aggressive return shot.

- SLICE and TOPSPIN—two different spins you can put on the ball when you make contact. For a slice, one cuts under the ball at contact to produce a shot that makes the ball stay low when it bounces on the opponent's side. For the topspin, one brushes up on the ball at contact to produce a shot that makes the ball bounce high on the opponent's side.

- POACH—a shot that's only applicable to doubles; when a frontcourt player cuts across the center of the court and intercepts a shot intended for the backcourt player or the player charging the net; this puts opponent off balance; a great strategic play once partners learn when and how to execute it.

Stacy shakes her head at all this information, so Arthur decides to test her.

"Okay," he says. "You've just hit a crosscourt backhand lob. What kind of shot is that?"

Stacy thinks a moment, then says, "It's a shot from my backhand side—that's the side across my body or, in my case, my left side—played diagonally across the court but hit high and over the head of my opponent."

"Right," Arthur declares. "See, you know more than you thought."

Stacy still has a puzzled look on her face. "Maybe, but are you telling me that there are different swings for each of these shots?" she inquires.

"Oh, yes," Arthur replies. "In fact, there are different strokes that affect each one of these shots.

THE SHOT

HIT THE BALL WHERE THE OPPONENT IS NOT
OR FORCE AN ERROR. THERE ARE MANY DIFFERENT
SHOTS THAT WORK.

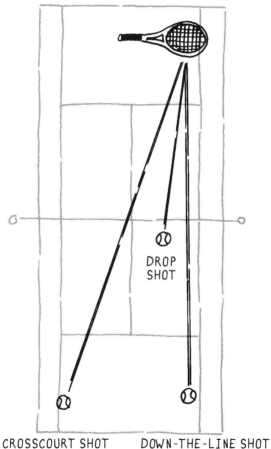

DROP
SHOT

CROSSCOURT SHOT   DOWN-THE-LINE SHOT

Don't worry; these are all things that will come to you as you practice, take lessons, and become more proficient on the court."

"Arthur," a voice calls from off the court. Stacy and Arthur look up to see Stephanie walking down the path toward them. "Ms. Wade is here for her lesson. She's early, and I told her you were tied up at the moment—"

"No, no," Stacy interrupts. "I don't want anyone waiting because of me. Besides, I think I'm ready to take a lesson and practice, practice, practice."

Arthur snaps his fingers, then points to Stephanie. "That's what I forgot," he exclaims. "I didn't go over where and how to practice." He looks back at Stacy and adds, "Tennis is a game that requires two people to play, but there are some ways to practice by yourself that will help you get ready for your big day."

Stephanie waves her hands and smiles a don't-worry-about-it smile. "You go give Ms. Wade her lesson," she tells Arthur. "I'll brief our other student here on the finer points of practicing."

EIGHT

HITTING THE COURTS

Once back inside the now-familiar confines of Stephanie's office, Stacy glances at the photos and posters with renewed interest and newfound confidence. She has yet to strike her first tennis ball, but she believes she won't make a fool of herself, nor is she likely to embarrass Matt. She gazes at a woman in one of Stephanie's posters and imagines herself in the middle of a point, pouring herself into the match, her steely eyes riveted to the ball, the court, and the moment.

"Stacy!" Stephanie speaks loudly.

"Yes," Stacy answers, jarred back to the present.

"I thought I'd lost you there for a second."

Stacy smiles. "Sorry, I was daydreaming. This is all very exciting to me."

"That's wonderful," Stephanie says. "Now, all we have to do is put that information into practice and you'll be on your way to center-court stardom. Which brings us to your dilemma. Where do you plan to play and practice?"

"I have no idea. This is the first tennis center I've ever visited, and I just happened to wander past here. I don't even know where my tournament is going to be held. What do I do?"

Stephanie outlines several options:

- First, she could join a PRIVATE CLUB, like Saddle Ridge, where all the practice facilities and equipment are at members' disposal. They have leagues, tournaments, and all sorts of activities, along with a staff of professionals who give lessons, string racquets, and schedule events. Private clubs offer a great social atmosphere, with all the amenities. The downside is the expense. Private clubs usually charge an initiation fee—a fee for joining—and monthly dues that go toward maintaining club facilities. In addition, they may charge for court time and certainly for lessons and, sometimes, equipment rental, like ball machines.

- An alternative to a private club is a PUBLIC-ACCESS, or SEMIPRIVATE CLUB. Many of these clubs have the same elaborate amenities; but rather than being strictly private, they open their facilities to the public on a for-fee basis. They have members, but at certain times others can pay a fee to play at the facilities. Again, the downside could be the expense.

- The same amenities are often available at a community recreation center or local park. These centers are either free or they charge a nominal court fee. They don't have the posh amenities or the exclusive environment of a private club, but for a good workout, there are plenty of parks and community centers that fit the bill perfectly.

- A fourth option requires some travel. Most RE-SORTS have world-class tennis facilities nestled in some of the most beautiful surroundings one can imagine. From Palm Beach to Palm Springs to Auckland, New Zealand, resort destinations have the best of all worlds, tennis included.

"I won't be flying to New Zealand to get ready for this tournament," Stacy observes in as dry a voice as she can muster. In fact, she knows which of the four options she's going to explore. There are plenty of parks and recreation centers in this city, and she plans to visit as many as necessary.

"You said something about renting equipment," she points out. "If I do choose to practice at an inexpensive public park, what sort of equipment will I need?"

"Remember," Stephanie says, "unless you're working on your serve, you can only practice by yourself with the help of practice aids. Tennis is a two- or four-person sport."

"So, what do I do?"

Stephanie discusses several choices:

- The most effective but most expensive way to practice alone is to rent a PNEUMATIC BALL MACHINE. These machines are mobile, hold over a hundred balls, and fire them out of an adjustable tube at the rate of one ball every

YOU CAN JOIN A PRIVATE CLUB,
PLAY AT SEMIPRIVATE COURTS,
PLAY AT PUBLIC PARKS, OR
TRAVEL TO RESORT DESTINATIONS.

three seconds. It's a great workout for ground-strokes and volleys. Of course, there are no breaks; you have to be ready. Pneumatic ball machines are fun, but they can be expensive to rent and hard to reserve.

- At a public park there's a lot of demand for the courts and for the practice equipment, so you should consider the wall or BACKBOARD. Lots of courts have one fence where a wall or back-board has been erected as a practice aid. These walls usually have a painted line denoting the height of the net, and they are positioned for solo practice in hitting the ball. It's a good workout for practicing technique and form but lacks the full effect of seeing where shots land.

- The most highly recommended teaching aid is a PRACTICE PARTNER, someone on the same playing level. Nothing can replace a real person returning real shots.

Stacy feverishly writes all her practice and playing options in her notepad, but she still has a few concerns. "What about when I'm at home," she inquires. "Is there anything I can do in my house or my yard to help my tennis skills?"

Stephanie suggests ways to improve eye-hand coordination and reaction skills:

- Just throwing and catching a ball against a wall at home can improve reaction skills.

- Learning to juggle two, three, even four tennis balls dramatically improves balance, concentration, and eye-hand coordination.

- Holding the racquet faceup and simply bouncing the ball up in the air on the racquet for extended periods of time increases ball control and provides a much better feel for the racquet.

"You can become the best juggler and ball bouncer in the city," Stephanie notes, "but that won't do you any good if you haven't spent time on the court working on your game."

Stacy nods. Point taken. "What about actually playing?" she asks. "Let's assume I play well enough in my upcoming tournament that I want to continue my tennis career. What do I do then?"

Stephanie leans forward. "Join a league," she insists, accenting each word. "Once you understand the game and can make contact with the ball enough times to finish a match, you need to join a neighborhood, club, or citywide league. You can join leagues through most park and recreation departments or through the local YMCA. Once you sign up, the league director will usually assign you to a team. In some instances, say, where citywide leagues are divided by districts, your district director will place you on a team with people who live near you. You will, of course, be ranked by ability, and you will play against players who are on your level. Your team then competes against other teams from your region. Depending on the league you join, you might travel across town or even to other towns to play some matches."

Stacy looks up from her notes. "Are you serious?"

PRACTICE TOOLS SUCH AS BALL MACHINES AND BACKBOARDS ARE GREAT, BUT NOTHING BEATS PRACTICING WITH OTHER PEOPLE.

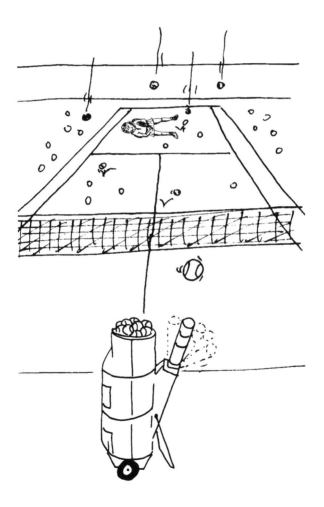

"Oh, yes," Stephanie continues. "In some cities leagues play year-round and teams travel as far as one hundred miles to play matches. It can be a very big thing. The Atlanta, Georgia, league, called ALTA—the Atlanta Lawn Tennis Association—has more than seventy-five thousand members. It's the largest tennis league in the world. That's an extreme example, but the point is that league play is a great way to make new friends in a healthy, competitive environment."

Stacy puts that on her short list of things to do. "Okay, are there any other drills or exercises or practice tips that might help me get ready for my debut?"

Stephanie walks to the door of her office. "Come with me," she says. "There's someone else you need to meet."

Stephanie leads her outside again, past the restaurant and the locker rooms, to a door at the far end of the clubhouse. When Stephanie opens the door, Stacy sees a gym filled with weights, treadmills, stationary bikes, and other workout equipment. Three women are perched on the bikes, peddling hard. A man is lying on a bench near the door. His hands grasp the bar above him and he lifts what looks like tons of weight. Stacy views all of this with interest. She still jogs, but she hasn't engaged in a serious workout routine since she and Matt were married.

"Horace!" Stephanie calls.

A door in the rear of the gym opens and a young, athletic man with strawberry blond hair and chiseled features steps out and walks toward them.

"Hi, Steph," he cries.

Stephanie motions toward Stacy. "Horace Decker, I'd like you to meet Stacy—"

"The lady who knows nothing about tennis," Horace blurts out.

"Word travels fast," Stacy comments.

"I understand you've had quite a day," Horace says.

Stacy holds up her notepad. "I've taken more notes today than I did in some of my college courses, but yes, I've learned a lot and had a great time. Everyone has been wonderful."

"Which is why we're here," Stephanie jumps in. "I was giving Stacy some practice tips and it occurred to me that she needs to be primed on working out and avoiding injuries."

Horace nods. "I have some time now."

NINE

TONED FOR TENNIS

Horace shows Stacy all the equipment in the Saddle Ridge gym, and he does his best to explain the exercise physiology behind each machine. After a brief tour of the workout and aerobic facilities, Stacy and Horace take a seat in metal folding chairs outside the door to Horace's small office.

"I really appreciate your taking the time to show me around," Stacy declares. "Now, about all this exercising. I don't intend to enter any Grand Slam events, and I'm not trying to be Mrs. Universe, but if there are some things I can do to prepare—"

"Yes, there are," Horace interrupts. "Tennis is an aerobic sport that combines all the elements of strength, coordination, speed, flexibility, and endurance. No one of these is more important than the other. By working on all these elements, you can improve your game and avoid a lot of common injuries that occur in tennis."

The word *injury* gets Stacy's attention. "What sort of workout do you recommend?" she asks.

Horace thinks for a moment before answering: "The most important thing about preparing for tennis or any other sport is balance and moderation. Don't focus on one aspect of your workout routine and neglect all others. The essentials for good tennis aren't mutually exclusive disciplines. They must work together to form a balance. Only then can you reach your full potential as a player."

"What sort of balance?" she wants to know.

"Take strength, for example," he says, pointing to some of the weight equipment. "Sure, strength is important in tennis, as it is in all sports; however, if you concentrate solely on strength, you might end up with the most powerful serve in the game but without the stamina, coordination, and flexibility to match.

"The same is true with speed. You might have the greatest foot speed in town, and you might be able to cover the court better than anyone else, but if you don't have enough strength to hit a quick, re-sounding return or if you don't have enough coordination to place your shots in play, what's the use?

"Endurance is equally important. It doesn't matter how well you play or how strong you are, if you don't have enough endurance to last the entire match, you're going to lose. Proper balance of all physical elements is the key to success. A proper blend of exercises and drills will prepare you for your day on the court."

Stacy flips to the last few pages of her notepad and lists the elements Horace has named. "Okay, Horace, I'm not going to spend the next thirty days of my life in the gym, and I'm not interested in running in a marathon, but I do want to be as prepared as I can be. Give me the abbreviated version of a good workout routine."

Horace smiles and nods. "Let's start with strength," he says. "You might think that tennis strength is simply arm strength or leg strength, since you are swinging the racquet with your arm and moving from shot to shot with your legs, but that kind of thinking would be wrong in the extreme. When you are using proper technique, you are using all the muscles in your body as part of the stroke. Your abdominal muscles, your back muscles, your arms, legs, chest, and shoulders all work together in a properly executed swing. As such, your strength training should be a total body workout."

For starters, he suggests:

- Work on standard body-resistant exercises to build strength. Sit-ups, pushups, leg lifts, and step training provide a good intro to more advanced strengthening exercises. They are simple exercises that can be done at home.

- After becoming comfortable with those exercises, progress to weight training. But be careful. It's very easy to overdo it when first starting to work out with weights. Lifting too much weight will strain muscles and cause injuries, while lifting too little weight won't provide the benefits being sought. Before embarking on a weight training program, talk to a trainer and a tennis pro.

- Another possibility is to work out on a stair machine or a climber. These isometric exercise machines provide constant resistance, increasing strength and stamina.

"The important thing to remember in setting your workout regimen is not to overdo it," Horace cautions. "In each exercise, find out what your maximum number of repetitions is and work with no more than half that number of reps. Take breaks of no less than thirty seconds and no more than one minute between different exercises. Also, work through your full circuit of exercises in one session."

"I haven't lifted weights in a long time," Stacy observes in a leery voice.

Horace takes away her concern, saying: "Don't feel like you have to lift weights if you aren't comfortable with it. Remember, no matter what kind of workout you choose, seek professional guidance and talk with your tennis pro about it."

"Okay," Stacy agrees, knowing that pushups, sit-ups, and leg lifts will probably be the extent of her strength training for the time being.

"What about flexibility?" she asks.

"It's crucial," Horace replies. "Muscle pulls and strains are the most common form of tennis injury. A good number of these could have been prevented by going through a regular stretching routine.

"There are a number of very good stretching exercises that will prepare you for tennis, but keep in mind, just like working out with weights, overdoing it in the early stages can lead to more problems than solutions."

He suggests some stretching exercises she should try to include:

- Touch your toes. This stretches the hamstring and hip muscles. The recommended way to do this is by sitting on the ground and reaching for your toes while keeping your back straight. Make it a sustained stretch without bouncing, and hold it for at least fifteen seconds. Don't panic if you can't reach your toes.

- The calf and Achilles pull will help loosen the most used and the most overlooked muscle group in your body: the calf muscles. Standing three feet from a wall with your feet flat on the floor, lean slowly into the wall until you feel a stretch, using your hands as a brace. Don't worry if you can't quite reach the wall, remember to hold *all* stretches for fifteen seconds, and don't overdo it.

- For other leg muscles such as the front upper thigh muscles, slowly go down on one knee while keeping your back straight and your head up. This exercise also helps develop better balance. Don't worry if you fall the first few times you try this one. It's common.

- For upper body stretching, clasp your arms behind your back and pull them upward. This will help improve your reach as well as loosen your arms.

- Another good stretching exercise is the old broom-handle turn. Take a broomstick or other long straight object and place it across your shoulders, holding each end with your hands. Keeping your lower body still, turn the broomstick by rotating your shoulders as far as you can in both directions. *Start slowly.* Once you're comfortable with this exercise, try doing it while sitting in a chair, to ensure that your lower body is still and your shoulders and torso are stretching around it.

Stacy glances up from her writing to make sure Horace has finished. "Wow, that's quite a list," she exclaims.

"Yes, it is, but it's very important. Staying loose and flexible will keep you active and on the court longer. Believe me, cramped or pulled muscles are no fun. Stretching can go a long way toward preventing them."

Stacy dutifully notes that point of wisdom. "Okay, what about speed and endurance? I jog a mile or so every other day. Does that help?"

"Of course it does," Horace assures her. "The longer you can sustain your runs, the more endurance you're building. To build tennis endurance it also helps to practice running sprints. These are quick bursts when you give it everything you have for a short run; then jog for a while before bursting into another full-blown sprint.

"Also, to work on your foot speed, you can practice running from side to side on the court. This will give you a sense of the stopping and starting you might experience during a match, and it will help you cover all sides of the court. Of course, other activities such as biking, swimming, skating, and skiing help build endurance and coordination. Anything that gets you in better shape will help your game.

"The one thing that probably won't get you into good shape is tennis itself. If you haven't built a fitness foundation before getting to the courts, don't expect to 'play' yourself into tennis shape. It won't happen."

"Horace, are there any injuries I should know about?" she wants to know.

"Probably the most infamous catchall injury you'll hear about is tennis elbow," he responds. "Actually, it's become so common that anyone who suffers any soreness anywhere near the elbow joint claims to have tennis elbow, and it needs to be examined by a doctor. Tennis elbow, which involves inflammation on the outside of the elbow, is tendinitis of the extensor tendons, resulting from overuse."

Horace goes on to explain that almost all injuries in the elbow region, whether it's common bursitis or tennis elbow, result from either poor technique, a racquet that's too stiff, or the string tension being too tight. Changing your form and using proper equipment not only can change your game, it can keep you healthy.

"Remember to work out in moderation," Horace summarizes. "Don't overdo it, but set a regular routine and stick to it. You can improve your game and yourself by staying fit. Also, don't drink alcohol. Tennis is a social game and it's very tempting to go out after a match and have a couple of drinks with your friends, but alcohol drains your body of the essential fluids and nutrients you need. Replenish your body with water or juice.

"Finally, remember that the will to win is not as important as the will to prepare to win."

After that tidbit of wisdom, Stacy thanks Horace and bids him a good day.

"Not so fast," he says as she's rising to leave. "I want to make sure you've covered all the bases before you leave here today."

Stacy looks down at her full notepad and takes inventory of everything she has learned, trying to figure if there's another area of learning she needs to pursue. "Can you think of anything else?" she asks Horace.

"Do you know the rules?"

"A little, I guess," she says, unsure where he's going with this.

"How about etiquette? Do you know how to behave yourself?"

"I hope so," Stacy affirms with a chuckle.

Horace raises his index finger in a wait-one-moment gesture. He stands up and walks to a door connecting the gym with the men's locker room. After disappearing for a moment, he comes out with the man Stacy saw lifting weights earlier. "Stacy," Horace says, "I'd like you to meet John Napkinroe, a member and our resident stickler on tennis rules and behavior."

EXERCISES

STEP-UPS

SIT-UPS

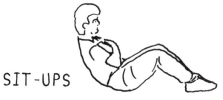

PUSHUPS

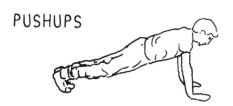

Both men laugh, and Stacy joins in. "Nice to meet you, John," she remarks.

"The pleasure's mine, Stacy. I understand from Horace that you're interested in learning the rules and etiquette of tennis. Why don't you let me buy you a soda? I think a short briefing on rules and etiquette should round out your day nicely."

Stacy thanks Horace again as she follows John out of the gym toward the restaurant where she is about to learn tennis's code of conduct from a master.

TEN

CROSSING THE LINE

John and Stacy sit at the same table where Stacy and Betty had lunch. The same smiling waitress greets them, and John orders tea while Stacy asks for a lemonade. After some chitchat, John turns the discussion back to tennis.

"So you have a tournament coming up in a month and you don't want to embarrass yourself," he remarks.

"That's right. Before today I didn't even know which end of a racquet to hold. I've yet to strike my first tennis ball, but now I at least know enough to get started."

John nods and sips his tea before speaking. "It's good to know you're so conscientious. Sure, you can get started quickly and have a lot of fun while you're learning, but you also need to be aware of those around you and be sensitive to the subtleties of tennis etiquette.

"Since you understand how the game is scored, let's start by talking about how the game is called."

"Called?" Stacy asks.

"Yes. I'm sure you've watched basketball and football games where there are referees, and baseball games where umpires are in charge of calling and administering the rules. Well, tennis is the same way. At the professional and top amateur level, tennis matches are called and ruled by a group of UMPIRES, REFEREES, LINESMEN, and JUDGES. Each of these folks has a role and a position during a match.

"An umpire is in charge of each match. His job is to make sure the rules of tennis are followed, the net is the correct height, and all faults and points are announced accurately. He makes sure the changeovers (when players switch ends of the court) are made appropriately, and he ensures fair play and proper decorum. An umpire's ruling is final, and he can overrule any calls made by judges or linesmen if he feels a mistake has been made. An umpire can even disqualify a player for unsportsmanlike conduct, a rule which, in my opinion, doesn't occur frequently enough. Anyway, the umpire sits in a chair on a high perch outside the doubles sideline at CENTER COURT."

John continues to explain the duties of officials. In overall charge of a tournament is the referee, whose job is to run the event for the executive committee or whatever sponsoring body is putting it on. The referee might not see a single match, and he is in no way a second umpire. He does, however, appoint and assign the umpires, judges, and linesmen, and he is the final authority. For instance, he decides when to call a rain delay.

Linesmen on the court during a match are assigned to watch each shot on one line and rule on whether or not a shot was in or out of the court. In professional tennis the ball is traveling well over one hundred miles an hour and a good number of the shots are close to if not on the line. It's such a tough task that major events sometimes have as many as eleven linesmen per match covering all the service lines, sidelines, and baselines. They normally sit in chairs outside the playing area but along the line they are covering. When a shot is out, a linesman will loudly call, "*Out!*" Disputes frequently arise and players appeal to the umpire. Sometimes the umpire overrules a linesman's call and sometimes he doesn't, but the decision of the umpire is final.

Matches are also called by judges, both NET JUDGES and FOOT FAULT JUDGES. A foot fault judge is positioned outside the playing area looking straight down the baseline. His job is to determine if a server's foot crosses the plane of the baseline or the plane of the centermark during the serve. If it does, he calls, "Fault!" The net judge is positioned at the net to determine whether or not a served ball strikes the net cord. When that happens, he calls "Let!" In some tournaments today the net judge has been replaced by a sensor that beeps when a served ball touches the net cord.

The final group of people you'll find on the court are the BALL BOYS and BALL GIRLS, who fetch errant balls after points or faults. They keep the pace of the game going by getting balls out of the way and making sure the server has balls when a point is ready to be played.

"Wow!" Stacy interjects as she calculates the number of all the people surrounding the court. "I bet it gets crowded out there."

"It can," John admits. "However, you probably won't see that many people around a match, unless you stun us all by becoming a Grand Slam finalist."

Stacy laughs and tells John that beyond this one small tournament, her goals are modest at best.

"Then you can expect to call all your own matches," John advises her. "That means you and your opponent are responsible for making all the line calls and net calls. It's sort of like calling your own fouls in a pick-up basketball game."

He then outlines some basic ground rules:

- If any portion of a ball hits the line, the shot is in. For a shot to be called out, the entire ball must hit outside the line.
- Often a player is on the opposite side of the court and cannot tell if a shot is in or out. If there is *any* question, then the shot is ruled in. Leave yourself no room for error, and you will defuse any uncomfortable disagreements before they occur.
- Always call the score before serving. It's the server's responsibility to keep score in the absence of an umpire. After a game, the server should call out how the match stands.

- Never serve until your opponent is ready. If you do, she doesn't have to return the serve and the point will not count, but neither will it count as a fault if your serve is out. As a receiver, when you're not ready on the serve, hold up your hand in a stop position and say, "Not ready."

Stacy writes down these rules, then takes a sip of her drink. "I want to do what's right," she says. "Are there any points of etiquette I should know?"

John mentions three:

- Never do anything to intentionally distract your opponent. Don't talk during your opponent's shot, and don't make any unruly or unnecessary yells, grunts, or gestures during a point.
- Coaching is against the rules. Don't give any instruction or advice, and don't accept any during a match.
- Avoid gamesmanship theatrics, like being intentionally slow between points or pointing and taunting your opponent. While these ploys aren't against the rules per se, they're in bad taste and they're juvenile. If you can't win with your racquet, lose gracefully.

"I would never consider doing something like that," Stacy blurts out.

"Good. If that's the case, there are some touring professionals who could take a lesson from you. It's unseemly, but some professionals will do anything, including intentionally gaming their opponents, in

order to win. It's conduct unbecoming to a professional, in my opinion."

"It's unbecoming to anyone," Stacy interjects.

John smiles and says, "With that sort of attitude,
you needn't worry about embarrassing yourself.
You'll do fine."

"I hope so," Stacy says. "Are there other rules I
need to remember?"

He describes some additional rules of etiquette:

- Before you arrive at a court, know the local
  rules of the club where you're playing. They
  might have specific dress policies like all-white
  or collared shirts, or there could be some restrictions on the times you can play. It's a good
  idea to call ahead.

- Regardless of where you're playing, it probably
  won't be a grandstand-lined stadium. There
  will be other courts with other matches going
  on right next to you. This leads to all sorts of
  awkward situations. If, during a point, there is
  any interference, like a dog running out onto
  the court or a ball from another match flying
  into your court, you should stop immediately
  and replay the point. Announce, "Ball on the
  court," or "Interference," to let your opponent
  know what has happened.

- Never step onto another court while someone
  else is playing. You could be hit by a ball, and you
  could disrupt a point in someone else's match.

- Be cognizant of your surroundings. If a match
  is going on right next to you, be courteous to

those people, just as you hope they will be to you. Don't yell or cheer while another match is going on, and don't move around in someone's field of vision while a point is being played.

• Most tennis etiquette rules are just rules of common sense and general decency. Treat others the way you hope they will treat you, and always try to be fair and courteous to everyone.

Stacy closes her notepad. "I can't thank you enough," she says.

"You'll be great," John responds. "I think you're going to find tennis to be a rewarding experience. It's also a great vehicle for building relationships. It's a game you can build on forever.

"Oh, by the way," John remarks as they stand to leave. "I have a little something that might help you later on."

He reaches into his bag and pulls out a small pamphlet. "Here is a glossary of tennis terms I've been carrying around for over a year. It could be helpful if you hear a word or a phrase you don't understand."

"This is wonderful," Stacy says. "I don't know how I can repay everyone at Saddle Ridge for all you've done today."

"You can go out there and win," John announces.

ETIQUETTE

NEVER DO ANYTHING TO
INTENTIONALLY DISTRACT
YOUR OPPONENT.

DON'T TALK DURING YOUR
OPPONENT'S SHOT, AND DON'T MAKE
ANY UNRULY OR UNNECESSARY YELLS,
GRUNTS, OR GESTURES DURING A
POINT.

COACHING IS AGAINST THE RULES.
DON'T GIVE ANY INSTRUCTION OR
ADVICE, AND DON'T ACCEPT ANY
DURING A MATCH.

ALSO, AVOID GAMESMANSHIP
THEATRICS, LIKE BEING
INTENTIONALLY SLOW BETWEEN
POINTS, OR POINTING AND TAUNTING
YOUR OPPONENT. THESE PLOYS AREN'T
AGAINST THE RULES PER SE, BUT
THEY'RE IN BAD TASTE AND THEY'RE
JUVENILE. IF YOU CAN'T WIN WITH
YOUR RACQUET, LOSE GRACEFULLY.

ELEVEN

THE NET RESULT

Several months later Matt arrives home early and finds that Stacy is out again. He had hoped to take her out to her favorite Italian restaurant for dinner. The phone rings while he's thumbing through the mail. It's one of Stacy's friends wondering if she's available for doubles tomorrow afternoon. Matt tells the friend that Stacy is out, but he assures her he will forward the detailed message. Then he checks the answering machine and hears another four calls for Stacy, all about tennis. Just then Stacy bounds into the house, her tennis bag in one hand and a large trophy in the other.

"What's that?" Matt asks.

"I won, Matt!" she cries with more excitement than he's heard in her voice in years. "I can't believe it. Our team is in the area finals, and I won the C division of our regional tournament. I won! Isn't it great?"

She holds out the trophy for Matt to examine.

He looks at the trophy, then back at his wife still dressed in her league tennis outfit. She's come a long way from that moment six months ago when she first learned she needed to take up tennis. Not only did she dazzle all of his coworkers during the office tennis tournament, she hasn't missed a single week of lessons. And she is in the running to win the most-improved-player award in the citywide tennis league she talked Matt into joining.

The phone rings nightly with friends trying to set up tennis dates, and they've met so many new people in the last four months that he has started carrying notecards in his pocket to help him remember all the new names. Now, staring at his wife's first tennis trophy, he's struck by how much their lives have changed as a result of a game.

"It's wonderful, honey. I'm very proud of you."

She wraps her arms around his neck and kisses him. "I love you, Matt," she says.

"I love you too, Stacy. How about we go out to dinner and celebrate?"

"Great. Let me shower, and I'll be ready to go."

While Stacy is getting dressed, Matt clears off one of the shelves in their bookcase and places the trophy front and center. It's a small bronze C-division singles trophy for an area league tournament; but as far as Stacy and Matt are concerned, it might as well be the silver U.S. Open cup.

Twelve

Napkinroe's Glossary

ace. A winning serve that is untouched or barely touched by the receiver.

ad court. The left service court as viewed from a player's baseline perspective. The left court is always the service court when the score is advantage.

ad-in. In most informal or non-officiated play, the way the score is called when the server has the advantage.

ad-out. In most informal or non-officiated play, the way the score is called when the receiver has the advantage.

advantage, or **ad.** The point after deuce. The player who has the advantage must win the next point to win the respective game.

all. An even score, a tie at any point, or a game other than deuce. Example: 30-30 is called 30-all.

alley. The four-and-a-half-foot-wide rectangular additions added to each side of the singles court for doubles play.

approach shot. A midcourt shot hit and followed to the net in hopes of hitting a volley for a winner.

ATP. Association of Tennis Professionals, an organization of male touring pros known for its weekly computer rankings of the world's top players and for representing the players' interests.

Australian Open. One of the four major tennis championships known collectively as the Grand Slam. The Australian Open is usually played in January.

babalot. The most expensive and desirable gut strings available in the game. Many of the top pros use it.

backboard. A wall or board erected along a fence to be used as a practice tool by a player practicing alone.

backcourt. The area between the service line and the baseline, often referred to as "no-man's-land" because of its strategic undesirability as a place from which to play.

backhand. A stroke played from the side of the body opposite the hand holding the racquet, i.e., a shot from the left side of a right-handed player, or a shot from the right side of a left-handed player.

ball. The round object hit back and forth over the net in tennis. Tennis balls must be more than two and a half inches, but less than two and five-eighths inches in diameter, and more than two ounces, but less than two and one-sixteenth ounces in weight.

ball boy. A male youngster (although there is no

official age limit) who fetches errant balls during a match. Ball boys stand in strategic locations around the court, two at the net and two at the fence, to minimize their influence on the match but to maximize their ability to retrieve balls efficiently. (*See also* **ball girl.**)

ball caddie. *See* **basket.**

ball girl. A female youngster who performs the same duties as a ball boy.

ball machine, or **pneumatic ball machine.** A practice tool, this device shoots balls out of an adjustable tube at a preset rate that can be adjusted up to one ball every three seconds. This allows a player to practice hitting shots alone.

ball mark. The impression left by a ball on clay, sometimes used by players calling their own lines to determine if a shot is in or out.

ball retriever. *See* **pick-up tube.**

ball toss. The act of throwing the ball with the hand in preparation of hitting a serve.

baseline. The court's back line that runs parallel to the net and perpendicular with the sidelines.

baseliner. A player or style of player where the player stays at or behind the baseline and plays a steady game of groundstrokes.

basket, or **ball basket,** or **ball caddie.** A large mesh container that holds practice tennis balls.

block. A short, punched ground stroke used to return a hard-hit shot.

bloomers. Female tennis pants, normally worn beneath a short tennis skirt.

break. Shortened version of service break, which is the loss of a game being served. A player is deemed to have broken serve if he or she wins a game while receiving serve from his or her opponent.

break point. The advantage point for the receiver, which, if won by the receiver, will result in a break. If the receiver is up two or three points in a game, she is said to have double or triple break points respectively; that is, she has two or three opportunities to break her opponent's serve.

break serve. Winning a game while opponent is serving.

bridge. The section of the racquet head between the shoulders of a split shaft.

butt, or **butt end, of the racquet.** The enlarged end of the grip, usually covered by a cap to provide support for the pad or heel of a player's hand.

bye. An empty position on a draw that allows a player to advance to the next round without actually playing a match. Such player is said to have drawn a bye.

center court. The premier grandstand-lined court, usually reserved for the top players' matches and most matches from the quarterfinals to the finals of major competitions. Also, an area on or near the center of any court. Tennis's equivalent to the fifty-yard line.

centerline. The line that separates the ad (left) and deuce (right) service courts.

centermark. The baseline hash mark that denotes the center of the baseline and establishes the barrier where a server must stand when delivering a serve.

center net strap. A singular white strap that runs from the top to the bottom of the net at its center, which maintains the net at its required three-foot center height.

certified pro. A teaching professional who has undergone rigorous training and development and has become a certified instructor by one of tennis's professional organizations.

change balls. A procedure in tournament tennis (not a rule) where balls are changed before the beginning of a third set. In professional tennis the first ball change is at either seven or nine games and all subsequent ball changes are at either nine or eleven games, with the number of games at a tournament's discretion. Note that the first ball change is made earlier because the first balls are also used for the five-minute warm-up, which is counted as two games.

change sides. After each odd-numbered game, players change ends of the court to equalize sun, wind, and other playing conditions.

chip shot. A softly hit shot intended to fall just over the net and down at the opponent's feet.

chip and charge. To hit a slice shot and then storm the net.

clay. One of the many surfaces found on tennis courts around the world. Clay courts are granular and considered slower surfaces than grass or hard courts. The French Open, one of the four Grand Slam events, is played on clay.

coaching. Advice given by an instructor or counselor. Coaching is strictly prohibited during a match under the Rules of Tennis.

code of conduct. Formal rules of etiquette during competitive play. Most major events provide for three stages of misconduct from competitors, the first stage resulting in a formal warning, the second stage resulting in a point penalty, and the third stage resulting in default of the match.

composites. Combinations of molded synthetic materials used in the construction of racquet frames.

Continental. One of the three basic grips in tennis, commonly characterized as a neutral grip—when the V of the hand gripping the racquet is pointed toward the sternum.

cord, or **net cord,** sometimes called **tape.** The tape that covers the top of the net and runs the entire length of the net.

court. The rectangular surface on which the game is played. The dimensions of the court are seventy-eight feet by thirty-six feet for doubles play and seventy-eight feet by twenty-seven feet for singles play. The court is bisected by the net, and court surfaces range from clay to grass to synthetic hard surfaces to, in rare instances, wood, carpet, and other materials.

court coverage. A player's ability to move quickly around the court to reach a variety of shots.

court fee. A rental fee for the use of a tennis court during a prescribed period of time.

court speed. The frictional effect a particular court surface has on a tennis ball. On "fast" surfaces the ball skids or rebounds quickly off the court, while on slow surfaces the ball responds sluggishly off the surface. Grass or a slick indoor surface are considered the fastest competitive surfaces in play today, and clay is considered the slowest.

court time. A reservation for the use of a court during a prescribed time.

crank. An exceptionally hard shot, usually a serve where a player is said to have "cranked it up."

crosscourt. A diagonal shot from one side of the court to the opposite side of the opposing court.

crossover. In doubles play, when one player crosses the center line into his or her partner's side of the court to hit a shot.

cross strings. Horizontal strings on the racquet's head, running perpendicular to the shaft.

demo. Demonstrator equipment, usually racquets, that pro shops lend on a trial basis for a limited period of time.

deuce. A tie game when each player has won three points. To win the game, a player must win two consecutive points from deuce, the first point being the advantage or ad and the second point being called the game. If the player with the ad loses the point, it goes back to deuce.

deuce court. The right service court as viewed from a player's baseline perspective. The right court is always the service court when the score is deuce.

dink. A softly hit shot. Someone who hits really soft is a "dinker."

double fault. When the server misses with both serves and, therefore, loses the point.

double hit. Striking the ball twice during the same stroke. If "intentional," a double hit results in the loss of the point. If unintentional and the stroke is one continuous motion, the double hit is allowed.

doubles. A two-on-two match, where two partners play two other partners on the wider doubles court, in accordance with Rules Governing the Doubles Game.

doubles alley. The lane or alley between the singles sideline and doubles sideline.

doubles posts. The outside posts on a court that are three feet, six inches high.

doubles sidelines. Outer sidelines beyond the singles sidelines that add four and a half feet to each side of the court.

down-the-line shot. A hit from one sideline to the other sideline in a straight direction.

draw. The lineup for how certain players are placed in the brackets of a tournament. After the appropriate seedings are made, the remaining players are placed by the draw, ostensibly a blind draw by lot.

drive. A firmly struck fast shot that bores into the opponent's court.

drop shot. A soft shot intended to barely clear the net and land out of the opponent's range or to draw the opposition into the net area, keeping the opponent off balance in order to set up the next shot.

Eastern. One of the three basic grips in tennis: when the hand gripping the racquet is positioned so that the V of the hand is pointed toward the right shoulder (right-handers).

equipment bag, or **pro bag,** or **tournament bag.** A lightweight but durable bag large enough to carry racquets, balls, and all other accessory items.

elliptical. Oval-shaped racquet head.

error. A mistake, usually referred to as "forced" or "unforced" error, meaning one player forced her opponent into making a mistake, or the opponent made the mistake on her own accord.

etiquette. *See* **code of conduct.**

face. The interior portion of the racquet head where strings are laced. The area of the racquet designed to strike the ball.

fault. Failing to put the ball into play with the serve.

fiberglass. One of many composite materials used in the construction of racquet frames.

fifteen. The first point won in a game.

first flight. The trajectory of a ball from the time it touches the racquet until it first touches the court.

follow through. The continuation and finish of the racquet after the ball has been struck.

foot fault. A failure to serve while both feet are behind the baseline and on the appropriate side of the centermark.

foot fault judge. An official, strategically positioned on the baseline during a match, who determines if and when a foot fault occurs.

footwork. The small steps taken before a shot to help the player get in position to strike the ball.

forecourt. The area between the net and the service line. The zone in which a volleyer normally plays.

forehand. The stroke from the same side of the body as the hand holding the racquet, i.e., a shot from the right side of a right-handed player, and a shot from the left side of a left-handed player.

forty. The third point won in a game.

frame. The exterior body of the racquet, formerly made of wood, now made of graphite, aluminum, fiberglass, kevlar, titanium, or other composite materials.

framed. A shot hit off the frame of the racquet, also known as a shank.

French Open. One of tennis's four major championships known collectively as the Grand Slam or simply the Slam. The French Open is played in Paris in the spring.

game. A contest within a set, made up of a series of points. The points in a game are fifteen, thirty, forty, and game, and a player must win the game by two points.

Grand Slam, or **the Slam.** Winning all four of tennis's major championships: the Australian

Open, the French Open, Wimbledon, and the U.S. Open.

graphite. One of many molded materials used in the construction of racquet frames.

grass. Historically, the first of many types of court surfaces found today. Wimbledon, one of the four Grand Slam championships, is played on grass.

grip. (1) The method of holding the racquet, one of the basics learned in the early stages of tennis instruction. (2) The leather or synthetic wrap (different from the grip wrap) added to the racquet handle.

grip wrap, or **wrap.** An additional thin wrapping surrounding the handle of the racquet.

grommet strips. Plastic strips surrounding the exterior of the racquet head that protect the strings from premature wear.

groundstroke. A stroke hit from the backcourt after the ball bounces.

gut. Natural racquet string made from animal intestines.

hack, or **hacker.** An impolite slang expression for a below-average player.

half-volley. A shot that is struck a fraction of a second after the ball strikes the ground, much like a dropkick.

handle. The area of the racquet, normally covered by a leather or synthetic wrap, where a player places the hand and grips the racquet.

hard court. Court surfaces made from concrete, asphalt, and other similar paving and/or synthetic materials.

head. The oval or teardrop-shaped end of the racquet where strings are laced.

head heavy. A racquet where the relative weight of the head to the grip is heavier than standard.

head lite. A racquet where the relative weight of the head to the grip is lighter than standard.

hold serve. To win a game in which you are serving.

International Tennis Hall of Fame. A museum of tennis history and a recognized monument to all the greats of the game, situated in Newport, Rhode Island.

ITF. The International Tennis Federation, the recognized international ruling body of tennis and the governing body of the four Grand Slam events.

judges. Officials who call matches—these include both net judges and foot fault judges.

kevlar. One of many composite materials used in the construction of racquet frames.

kill. An overhead smash shot that is unreturnable.

left service court. *See* **ad court.**

let. The word used in the Rules of Tennis to denote a replay, primarily called when a serve hits the net cord and continues over the net and into the service court; officially used to mean any time a point or shot must be replayed.

liner. A shot that lands on the line and is, in accordance with the rules, a good shot.

linesmen. Officials strategically positioned around the court on the lines during a match to determine if shots are in or out of the boundaries of the court.

lingering death. A tiebreak method where the first player to reach seven in the tiebreak format wins; however, the player must win by two points.

lob. A shot lofted high in the air.

long. A shot that lands beyond the service line on the serve, or behind the baseline during the play of a point.

love. Zero, derived from the French word *l'oeuf,* meaning "egg."

main strings. Vertical strings of a racquet running lengthwise, perpendicular to the cross strings.

match. The overall contest, usually decided by the best two out of three or best three out of five sets.

match point. The point at which the player leading the match needs to win only one more point to win the match.

mixed doubles. A doubles match where each team consists of one male competitor and one female competitor.

nap. The woven downy-like material of a ball that covers the hollow sphere inside—affects the bounce of the ball.

National Tennis Rating Program (NTRP). The system that rates players numerically from a 2.5 (beginners who have certain basic skills) all the way to 7.0 (the best players in the world).

net. The mesh barrier bisecting the court and suspended at both ends by posts. The net is three feet, six inches high at the posts, and three feet high at the center.

net cord. *See* **cord.**

net judge. An official in a match, stationed strategically beside the net, who determines if a serve has touched the net.

net play. An aggressive style of play where a player rushes to the net to hit volleys and overheads, while trying to take control of the point by hitting a winner or forcing an error.

net post, or **post.** The permanent fixtures that hold the net in place at its prescribed three-feet, six-inch height on each side of the court.

net sticks, or **singles sticks.** The temporary sticks inserted into the net three feet outside the singles sidelines to bring the net up to the prescribed three-feet, six-inch height at both singles sidelines.

no-man's-land. The area in between the service line and the baseline, named such because it is an undesirable area from which to play.

open. A tournament in which both amateurs and professionals may compete.

overhead smash. A shot where the hit occurs above the player's head and the racquet is brought down in a fashion similar to a serve.

oversized. Larger head designs in racquets that affect a greater hitting area.

overwrap. An additional wrap placed over the grip either to make the grip bigger or to provide a softer feel.

passing shot. A shot hit past an opponent who has come up to the net.

pick-up tube. Device open in one end, used for

picking up tennis balls without having to stoop over. Holds fifteen to twenty balls.

placement. A shot aimed and struck with precision accuracy.

pneumatic ball machine. *See* **ball machine.**

poach. To cross over the center serviceline and intercept a shot meant for one's doubles partner, and then hit a volley.

point. The unit of measure on which a game, set, or match is based. Each engagement between competitors when a ball is put into play is called a point.

practice basket. A plastic woven basket with gaps between the bottom weaves large enough so you can force a ball through the openings without having to bend over. Holds up to thirty or more balls.

private club. A tennis facility that requires paid membership and is not open to the general public.

pro, or **tennis professional.** A person who accepts prize money for playing tennis; and/or teaches tennis for money; or profits from knowledge, experience, or actions within the game.

pro shop. A retail outlet specializing in tennis equipment, apparel, and accessories.

public-access club. A tennis club open to the public, although fees usually are charged. Memberships also usually are available.

pusher. A baseline player who methodically returns all shots in a defensive manner in the hope that his opponent will become impatient and make an error.

qualifying. Matches you need to play and win to get into the main draw of a tournament.

racquet. Primary piece of equipment in tennis. The elements of a racquet are the head, the shaft, the shoulders, the throat, the handle, the butt, and the strings.

racquet cover, or **racquet carrier.** A thermal bag with shoulder strap large enough to carry from one to six racquets.

rally. The exchange of shots during a point.

ranking. A player's standing, from best to not-the-best, compared with other players.

ready position. A posture of readiness for receiving a serve.

rebound. The reaction of a ball when it impacts another object like the court, a wall, or a racquet.

receive. Opponent is serving.

receiver. The player not serving during a game.

referee. The official empowered by the tournament committee or sponsoring body to rule in all matters regarding tournament play and playing conditions in accordance with the Rules of Tennis.

return-of-serve, or **return.** A term reserved for the shot following the serve.

reflex. A quick reaction to a closely hit shot, usually used when describing a quick round of volleys. Example: reflex volley.

resorts. Travel destinations offering what often are world-class tennis facilities nestled in some of the most beautiful surroundings imaginable.

return. A shot hit back to an opponent.

scrambler. A player who hustles to reach virtually every shot.

second flight. The trajectory of the ball after it has struck the ground and before it is returned.

seeding. The placement of certain players in certain positions within the brackets of a tournament so as to ensure that the two best players are in separate brackets and the best players are positioned to meet each other in later rounds.

semiprivate club. *See* **public-access club.**

serve, or **service.** The first shot of a point, executed when the server puts the ball in play by throwing the ball in the air with his hand and hitting it before it hits the ground from a prescribed location into a prescribed service court in accordance with the Rules of Tennis.

serve–and–volley. An aggressive style of play that many players prefer. By charging the net and hitting a volley, serve-and-volley players often hit quick winners.

service break. To win a game when one's opponent is serving. (*See also* **break.**)

service court. Smaller rectangular courts bounded by the net, the sideline, the service line, and centerline. Each side of the net has two service courts known as the deuce court and the ad court. Service alternates into each of these courts.

service line. The line marking the depth of the service courts and separating the forecourt from the backcourt.

service winner. An unreturned serve, although not technically considered an ace because the receiver makes contact but doesn't have a play on the ball.

set. A unit of scoring comprising as many games as necessary for a player to win at least six games by a margin of two games, unless a tiebreak rule has been instituted under the Rules of Tennis.

shaft. The portion of the racquet that connects the head with the grip.

shank. Hitting the ball off the frame of the racquet. A mis-hit.

shoulders. The areas of the racquet where a split shaft connects with the racquet head.

sideline. The lines defining the left and right outer margins of the court, and running perpendicular and connecting to the baselines.

singles sidelines. Inner sidelines of a tennis court depicting area for singles play.

singles sticks. *See* **net sticks.**

sitter. A ball that rebounds softly, and sits up for an easy put away.

Slam, or **the Slam.** *See* **Grand Slam.**

slice. Hitting at an acute angle underneath the ball, thus imparting backspin on the shot and keeping the ball lower.

smash. An overhead stroke hit much like a serve.

spin. (1) Pronounced rotation of the ball caused by the racquet's angle of attack. (2) The act of spinning a racquet to determine rights to choose service or court preference.

squared. Refers to type of racquet head that is squarish in shape.

stance. Set position and posture a player takes to prepare for hitting a serve or shot.

stiffness. The relative resistance that a racquet has to certain pressures.

string. The fine interwoven natural fiber or synthetic material that encompasses the hitting area of the racquet.

string-a-ling. Fine plastic dividers often inserted between the weaves of strings to protect the strings against friction.

string tension. An important variable in selecting a racquet, referring to the tightness of the strings.

sudden death. A tiebreak system of nine points, where the first player to reach five points respectively wins the tiebreak and the set.

sweet spot. The area on the racquet head, usually in the center, where the ball springs off the racquet cleaner and truer and with better feel.

teardrop. Refers to style of racquet head shaped like a tear.

tension. Normally used to describe the pounds of pressure used in stringing a racquet and the resultant stiffness of the strings.

thermal racquet bag. A carrying bag that can hold between one and six racquets, as well as other items. Usually padded, it has full-length shoulder straps for easy carrying around.

thirty. Second point won in a game.

throat. The open portion of the racquet between the head and the handle.

tiebreak. A system for deciding the winner of a tied set by either sudden death or lingering death in accordance with the Rules of Tennis.

topspin. The overspin imparted on the ball by the racquet's angle of attack, which makes the ball bounce higher.

tournament. A competition established to determine a winner through a series of matches.

tournament tough. Possessing the competitive stamina and tournament experience necessary to win a championship.

two-handed backhand. Hitting a backhand shot while gripping the racquet with both hands.

umpire. The ruling official of a match, in charge of keeping and calling the score.

U.S. Open. One of tennis's four major tournaments, known collectively as the Grand Slam. The U.S. Open is played on hard courts in New York in late summer.

USPTA. The United States Professional Tennis Association, an organizing and certifying body for teaching professionals.

USPTR. The United States Professional Tennis Registry, an organizing and certifying body for teaching professionals.

USTA. The United States Tennis Association, the governing body of American amateur tennis.

volley. To hit a shot before the ball hits the ground, usually from the forecourt area.

Western. A style of gripping the racquet handle whereby the V of the hand gripping the racquet is pointed well right of the right shoulder (for right-handers).

wide. A shot that lands outside the prescribed sidelines and is, therefore, not a good shot.

Wimbledon. The site of the Lawn Tennis Championships, one of tennis's four major tournaments, known collectively as the Grand Slam. Wimbledon is played on grass courts in early summer at the All England Tennis and Croquet Club in Wimbledon, England.

winner. An unreturned shot hit for the outright win of a point.

WTA. The Women's Tennis Association, the organizing body of women's professional tennis.